Stress handling and control as a function of reinforcement among type A individuals

By : Gupta, Mohan

CONTENTS

Sr. No	Chapter	Page no.
1.	Introduction	1 – 61
2.	Review of Literature	62 – 96
3.	Methodology	97 – 107
4.	Results	108 – 158
5.	Discussion	159 – 172
6.	Summary	173 – 185
7.	References	186 – 214

CHAPTER – I
INTRODUCTION

INTRODUCTION

Stress:

Stress in the twenty first Millennium? Not some thing new, not any thing unknown, stress has been experienced since time immemorial, but its toll is higher than ever before, with increasing complexity in our life style, the level of stress has been rising at a phenomenal rate. When we analyse visit to doctors 75 to 90 percent are for stress related problems (Pareek, 1999). The claims for stress are twice as high as these paid for non stress physical problems injury or disease. The factors that contribute to stress not only differ between cultures, but also with in a culture itself; from a sophisticated industrial society to foragers; and from upper class to lower class with in the same society. Life would be simple indeed if our needs were automatically gratified. As we know many obstacles, both personal and environmental prevent this ideal situation. Such obstacles place adjustive demands on individual and can lead to stress. The term stress has typically been used to refer both to adjustive demands placed on an organism and to organism's internal biological and psychological responses to such demands. Adjustive demands are the stressors, the effect they create within an organism is stress and the efforts to deal with stress are the coping strategies. Separating these constructs is a somewhat arbitrary action as Neufeld, (1990) has pointed out, stress is a byproduct of poor or inadequate coping.

Do we know the history of stress as we know about its geography? Like natural directions (East, West, South and North), stress too has four such directions. Stress is not something to avoid; in fact, it is impossible to do so. Complete freedom from stress is death (Selye, 1983). Selye distinguishes between two basic types of stress: eustress, which is pleasant, curative and often motivational, and distress, which is unpleasant or disease-producing stress.

What may be distress to one person may be eustress to another How a person responds to stress depends on a number of factors: the environment, the magnitude of the stressor, what has gone before, the person's perception of the situation and self perceived ability to handle the stressor, the person's physical condition and the person's previous pattern in dealing with the stressor (Benjamin, 1987).

Selye also adds two other types to the description of the stress of life. These are overstress (hyperstress), where we have extended the limits of adapt ability, and understress (hypostress), where we suffer from alack of self-realization, such as physical immobility, boredom, or sensory deprivation (Selye, 1983).

Which way is the wind of stress blowing- is it bringing with it a rain of tears (as in stress due to immense joy or deep grief), or a cyclone of rage and anger, or the cool relaxing sea breeze of equanimity in life? The geography of stress also reveals that there are regions: the torrid equatorial region characterized by suffocating heat generated by excessive stress; the temperate region marked by optimal temperature, humidity and breeze, that is, the region of stress arousal which is optimal for effective performance, and the polar region which could be well equated to the lowest levels of stress arousal, bringing in its wake boredom due to hypostress. Stress has a long history; in fact, it is as old as humankind itself.

As early as in the fourteenth century, the term stress was used to denote hardship, straits, adversity or affliction (Lumsden, 1981). In the late seventeenth century, Hooke (Hinkle, 1973; 1977) used the word stress in the context of the physical sciences.

According to Hinkle (1973) Hooke's Law defines load as the external force; stress is the ratio of the external force (created by the load) to the area over which the force is applied; and strain is the resultant deformation in the object. It is this idea which was adopted to understand the effects of load on individuals. If metals break down under constant overload how about individuals?

The analogy between man and material may be extended further. For instance, if a certain amount of load is applied to a piece of iron wire, the wire may remain unaffected. However, the same amount of force may overload a delicate silk fibre, causing it to break. Thus, the capacity of an object to withstand stress depends on its inherent characteristics: toughness, tensility and strength. Human beings are no different. The effect of stress varies widely from one person to another. Thus, whether a particular situation will be stressful for an individual or not, depends on the inherent characteristics of the individual.

Stress therefore lies in the eyes of the beholder, much like the redness of the apple, the blueness of the sky or the greenness of grass. Etymologically, the word stress is derived from the Latin word stringer meaning to draw tight. Could they have Chosen a better word? Probably not. This conjures up images of an individual with a noose around his neck: the noose of uneasiness and distress; the noose gradually tightening its hold, taking all in its grip, till it eventually strangulates the individual. Yes, this is exactly what happens if stress is left unleashed. Six centuries later, most of us are aware of tightness in the throat, increased breathlessness, the rush of blood to the face, butterflies in the stomach and other symptoms which are associated with most forms of stress.

Hinkle (1973) cites Sir William Osler' and his system is subjected to the stresses and strains, which seem to be the basic factor in so many cases of 'Angina Pectoris'. Much along the same lines, Walter B Cannon studied the effects of stress on human beings and animals in terms of the well-known 'fight or flight' syndrome. Under duress, human beings tend to choose between two alternatives: the first is to make all attempts to resist (i.e., fight) the environmental pressures and through that process emerge victorious. The second is to avoid the pressure (i.e., flight) through the use of a variety of defense mechanisms. This is their way of reducing the pressure. It was Cannon who first elaborated on the physiological basis of stress. He observed that individuals experiencing extreme heat or cold, lack of oxygen, or excitement tended to show increased levels of adrenaline secretion. He described such people as being under stress.

Selye recognised that stress has great adaptive value, and labeled the stress response as the General Adaptation syndrome (GAS). It has recently been suggested (Melhuish, 1978) that stress is as much a product of evolution as any other biological mechanism. For human survival to be possible in a predominantly hostile environment, some mechanism was required to enable a quick response to physical dangers. As Cartwright and Cooper (1977) put it, 'the body developed the ability to rev up for a short time'. This mobilisation of physical forces is none other than Cannon's Fight or Flight reaction or Selye's GAS. However, the problem today is that whereas primitive man had ample opportunities for sublimating the excess energy generated (i.e., in the flight against predators for survival), modern man does mobilise the extra resources but has no way to cathart them. Neither fight nor flight is feasible in the physical sense of the word today.

A number of researchers have advocated individual differences approach to the study of stress (e.g., Haggard, 1949; Lazarus, 1966; Opton and Lazarus, 1967; Selye,

1975). One of the pioneers of the individual differences approach to stress (Haggard, 1949) wrote almost fifty years ago that some of the factors which influence an individual's ability to tolerate and master stress include: the nature of his early identifications and his present character structure and their relation to the demands and gratification of present stress producing situation. The appropriate understanding of the role of individual differences as co-determinants of the phenomenon of stress was possible due to approaches to stress development in 1960-1970s. Of most significance was Lazarus (1966), Opton and Lazarus (1967) contribution. There exist an enormous number of factors that, in interaction with each other, determine the individual specific components of stress (Strelau, 1989). Among the many determinants of individual differences considerable attention was devoted to personality characteristics. The later have been considered as moderators of stress (Folkman and Lazarus, 1988). The level of stress depends partly on a stressor's characteristics and partly on a person's resources, both, personal and situational, and the relationship between the two. Everyone faces a unique pattern of adjustive demands. This fact is partly due to differences in the way people perceive and interpret the situations. Person's perception and tolerance of stress, external resources and social support, and the nature of the stressors are some of the important factors that determine the level of the stress.

Aggarwal (2001) elucitidated the following facts regarding stress :

1. Too little or too much stress (i.e., hypostress or hyperstress) is bad. An optimal level of stress, varying from individual to individual, is good and necessary.

2. Stress can be due to both pleasant and unpleasant events. The goal should be to strike a balance between the equally destructive forces of hypostress and hyperstress. At the same time, one should try to maximise eustress and minimise distress.

3. Stress is dependent on the individual's cognition of the events.

4. Stress can be seen in individuals who are not facing any intensely emotional event. Rather, minor irritants or daily hassles of life may cause it, having a cumulative effect similar in nature to that caused by major traumatic events requiring large-scale adjustments to life.

5. Stress is an inevitable part of life, manifested universally as much in the East as in the West.

6. Stress does not invariably lead to a disease. There are a variety of ways to counteract the debilitating effects of stress.

7. The effects of stress are not always a function of variables such as age, sex and socio-economic status. It tends to cut across major demographic variables and it is this which increases it universality.

The Nature of stress

On the basis of these facts, certain conclusions may be drawn regarding the nature of stress. What is stress? It is clear that through everyone faces stress; it is difficult to define it. It is apparent that it is a phenomenon with the potential for manifestation anywhere in the world. For instance, a child, an adolescent, a girl, a boy, an adult, a house wife, an employee, an entrepreneur and a retired person face the debilitating effects of stress some time in their life. However, the same event that is stressful for one person may not at all be stressful for another. In order to produce stress, the event must be perceived as being stressful, i.e., as requiring resources or skills beyond the individual's capacity to deploy. Similarly, the effects of each event also depend upon the individual: while one person may prosper under such circumstances (for example, a highly taxing job), another may wither. The optimal level of stress varies from one individual to another. Events which are perceived as being stressful are not restricted to those causing major upheavals in life. The cumulative effects of minor irritants in one's daily routine can be equally stressful.

To sum up, stress is caused whenever any event, small or big, pleasant or unpleasant, internal or external, is perceived as making demands over and above the coping resources (Physical, social psychological, financial or even temporal) possessed by the individual.

Defining Stress

The conceptualization of stress by Selye is basically a physiological one, in which the stress response is seen as a necessary adjunct to the organism's fight for survival. By causing various body changes, the stress response prepares the individual for any exigency giving her extra resources to "fight" that emergency or to take 'flight' from it. At the same time, the term stress implies strain, which can be caused by prolonged exposure to the stressor. Coronary heart disease psychosomatic symptoms and premature aging may be some of the repercussions.

To define stress ideas can be taken from different sources (Mechanic 1976; Cox, 1978; Lazarus and Folkman, 1984 b; Singer and Davidson, 1986; Stotland, 1987; Trumbull and Appley, 1986). Stress is the condition that results when person/environment transactions lead the individual to perceive a discrepancy whether real or not between the demands of a situation and the resources of a person's biological, psychological and social systems. The four components of this definition need little elaboration:

1. Stress taxes the person's biopsychosocial resources for coping with difficult events or circumstances. These resources are limited.

2. The phrase 'demands of a situation' refers to the amount of our resources the stressor appears to require.

3. When there is a poor fit or a mismatch, between the demands of the situation and the resources of the person, a discrepancy exists. This generally takes the form of the demands taxing or exceeding the resources, such as when we have too much to do in too short a time. Opposite discrepancy also occurs, that is, our resources may be under utilized and this can be stressful too.

Our assessments of discrepancies between demands and resources occur through our transactions with the environment. These transactions are affected by many factors, including our prior history and aspects of the current situation.

Since the beginning of 1950s under the influence of Hans Selye's two most popular monographs (1950, 1956) hundreds of papers and books have been published with the aim of presenting different aspects of psychological stress. Hans Selye the grandmaster of stress research and theory said that stress, like relativity is a scientific concept, which has suffered from the mixed blessings of being too well known and too little understood.

When most people talk about stress it is usually in terms of pressure they are feeling from something happening in their immediate environment. Selye (1975) considered stress to be a physiological reaction that is entirely determined by stimuli intensity. In his later publications, in which more attention was paid to psychological phenomena, stimuli intensity was for him, the determinant of stress. It is immaterial whether the agent or situation we face is pleasant or unpleasant, all that counts is the intensity of the demand for readjustment or adaptation.

Stress has been conceptualized in three ways (Coyne and Holroyd, 1982; Stotland, 1987). One approach focuses on the environment, describing stress as a stimulus. Events or circumstances that we perceive as threatening or harmful, thereby producing feelings of tension are called stressors. Researchers who follow this approach study the impact of a wide range of stressors including (1) Catastrophic events, such as tornadoes and earthquakes, (2) major life events, such as the loss of a loved one or a job, and (3) more chronic circumstances such as living in crowded or noisy conditions.

The second approach treats stress as a response, focusing on people's reaction to stressors. The response has two interrelated components: the psychological component and the physiological component. The psychological component involves behaviour, thought pattern and emotions (example when you feel nervous). The physiological component involves heightened bodily arousal (examples your heart pounds, mouth goes dry, stomach feels tight, perspiration). The person's psychological and physiological response to a stressor is called strain.

The third approach describes stress as a process that includes stressors and strains, but adds an important dimension, the relationship between the person and the environment (Mechanic 1976; Cox, 1978; Lazarus and Launier, 1978; Lazarus and Folkman, 1984 a, 1984 b; Strelau 2001). This process involves continuous interactions and adjustments called transactions between the person and the environment, with each affecting and being affected by the other. According to this view, stress is not just a stimulus or a response, but rather a process in which the person is an active agent who can influence the impact of a stressor through behavioral, cognitive and emotional strategies. People differ in the amount of stress they experience from the same stressor.

Agarwala, Malhan and Singh (1979), believe that the confusion in definition is partly due to the fact that the same term is used variously by scholars of different disciplines. In physics, stress is a force, which acts on a body to produce strain. In physiology, the various changes in the physiological functions in response to evocative agents denote stress (rather than strain). In psychology, stress refers to a state of the organism resulting from some interaction with the environment. In psycho-physiology, stress is that stimulus which imposes detectable strain that cannot be easily accommodated by the body and so presents itself as impaired health or behaviour.

Ivancevich and Matteson (1987) define stress simply as the interaction of the individual with the environment. An adaptive response, mediated by individual differences and/or psychological processes, that is a consequence of any external (environmental) action, situation, or event that places excessive psychological and physical demands upon a person.

What purpose do models serve in any discipline? They serve exactly the same function as the architect's model of a prospective building. In exactly the same way, when a scientist draws up a model, he has certain goals in mind. What are these?

1. The model presents a holistic picture of the phenomenon under study. Thus, a model of stress presents a visual image of the stress phenomenon in totality: the causal factors, the symptoms and the process and the end result.

2. A model is generally amenable to graphical reproduction, in the form of a flow chart, outlining the sequence of events occurring in the phenomenon under study. As in all flow charts, which represent different stages of the phenomenon. The scientist may

explain the process using a linear model (unidirectional), or a complex interactional model with variables and stages influencing each other in both backward and forward directions. There may even be feedback loops to show the effect of the last stage on the ones preceding it, as in cyclical models.

3. Models are validated theories, a theory decides the avenues of research, and these research findings are then orchestrated in the model. Since models depict all parts of the phenomenon, they have an important function: they help the scientist to deal with the problem areas, in fact, to prevent problems from occurring.

A wide variety of models of stress has been presented over the years, ranging from models analysing just one aspect (say, organisational role stress) to those attempting to provide a general framework for the understanding of the stress phenomenon.

Aggarwal (2001) describe three main categories as of models of stress. Physiological models such as the General Adaptation Syndrome (GAS), (Selye, 1950). Load of information models, for example, Stimulus Overload/ Under load Model, for (Suedfeld, 1979), and Optimal Informational flow and Mood (Hamilton, 1981). Interactional models like Cognitive Model of Stress (Lazarus and Folkman, 1984).), and Systems model. (Lumsden, 1975).

The Physiological model or General Adaptation Syndrome

Hans Selye's General Adaptation Syndrome (GAS) has been widely held as a comprehensive model to explain the stress phenomenon. This three stage model states that when an organism is confronted with a threat, the general physiological response occurs in three stages

ALARM REACTION: The first stage includes an initial 'shock phase. in which resistance is lowered, and a 'counter-shock phase' in which defensive mechanisms become active. Alarm reaction is characterised by autonomous excitability' adrenalin discharge; increased heart rate, muscle tone, and blood content; and gastrointestinal ulceration. Depending on the nature and intensity of the threat and the condition of the organism, the periods of resistance vary and the severity of symptoms may differ from 'mild invigoration' to 'disease of adaptation

STAGE OF RESISTANCE: Maximum adaptation occurs during this stage. The bodily signs characteristic of the alarm reaction disappear. Resistance increases to levels above normal. If the stressor persists, or the defensive reaction proves ineffective, the organism deteriorates to the next stage.

STAGE OF EXHAUSTION: Adaptation energy is exhausted. Signs of the alarm reaction reappear, and the resistance level begins to decline irreversibly. The organism collapses.

Selye's remarks on his work on stress and the GAS clarify the general utility of any model of stress. For too long the models and theories have been considered to be only of academic interest. According to Selye, his work enabled him to develop a very satisfactory code of conduct. His model can be used to develop a universal code of conduct. Such a code postulates that one's adaptation energy is finite and should not be destroyed through overwork. The model can be used to design achievement through 'the pleasant stress of fulfillment i.e., Eustress, with out the harmful consequences damaging but inevitable stress or distress. The point of the code is not to abolish stress, but to master it. It is a matter of choosing, not an undemanding lifestyle, but a eustressfully rather than a distressfully damaging one.' Do not try to abolish stress, try to master it.

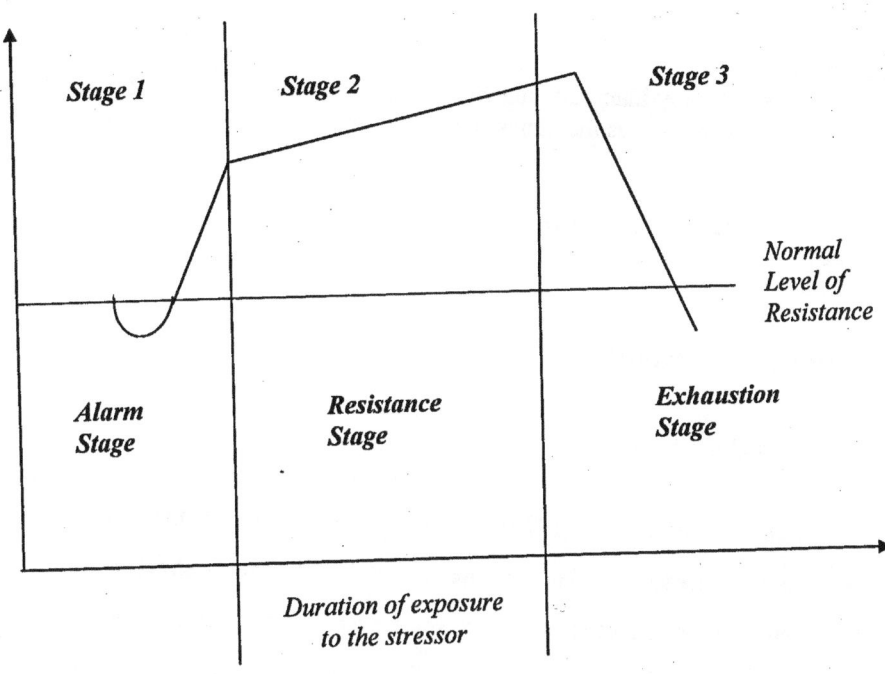

Figure 1 : A Brief Sketch of the Three Stages of the GAS

Shock Phase
- Immediate reaction
- Tachycardia, loss of muscle tone
- Decreased temperature
- Decreased blood pressure

Counter shock phase
- Rebound reaction
- Mobilisation of defensive phase
- Enlarged adrenal cortex
- Secretion of corticoid hormones
- Death results if stage persists

Resistance stage
- Full adaptation to stressor
- Improvement/disappearance of symptoms
- Adrenal cortex becomes rich in corticoid hormones
- If noxious agent persists, resistance and adaptation are lost.

Exhaustion stage
- As any inanimate machine breaks down under constant wear and tear so does the human body burn out.
- Burn out
- Disease
- Death if stage persists

Load of Information Models

Stimulus Overload/Underload Model

Proposed by Suedfeld (1979), it links stress not to the quality of environmental experiences (as in the Holmes and Rahe life events stress approach), but also to the structure of experiences. Thus, some events may be extremely aversive but may not involve stimulation levels outside the optimal zone. Conversely, events may be positive in nature, but their very bulk makes them stressful. In other words, too much of a good thing may be stressful. A U-shaped relationship is hyphothesised between stimulus load and stress, with stress being caused by both stimulus underload and overload.

Suedfeld has identified several factors considered important for the determination of the optimal level of stimulus load. While physiological arousal is crucial, personality variables such as locus of control, cognitive complexity and extraversion-introversion play an important role in the evaluation of the level of stimulation considered optimal by the person. Other determinates are age and educational level.

Optimal Information Flow and Mood

Proposed by Hamilton (1981), it is along the same lines as stimulus overload/underload model. It posits the same type of U-shaped relationship between optimal information flow and mood. Positive moods are an outcome of optimal information; negative moods (anxiety at the high end and boredom at the low and) reflect a mismatch between what is considered the optimal level and the actually available stimulation. Negative moods will impact behaviour negatively.

However, human beings are not totally in the hands of environmental stimulation. The susceptibility to such negative loads is monitored by what are called Attention Regulators. These attention regulators work as cognitive mechanisms and are under the voluntary control of the individual. Hence these Attention Regulators act to either augment or reduce the information available. Therefore it is one's own frame of mind which experiences the boredom in its environmental condition and if the boredom is extreme the information overload can be aversive and stressful.

Interactional models

These models focus on the relationship between the individual and the environment. The basis of the relationship is a cognitive one. In other words, one is mentally evaluating or appraising one's relationship with the environment. Thus, whether an event will be stressful or not, will depend, not on the objective characteristics of the event, but on the subjective perception of those characteristics. The common core of all such theories is that an imbalance or mismatch between two aspects causes stress: resources/capabilities/needs of the person, and demands/supplies made by the environment.

Cognitive Model of Stress

The Cognitive Model of Stress is proposed by Lazarus and Folkman (1984) who define stress as 'a particular relationship between the person as taxing or exceeding his or her resources and endangering his or her wellbeing'. On the basis of both laboratory and field studies, Lazarus and Folkman have evolved a model of stress incorporating three major issues:

The first issue involved the primary appraisal i.e. a process of event evaluation leading to positive or negative effects of the precision of stress by the individual. Thus an event which goes against the persons commitments is more likely to be perceived as being stressful than one which has no relevance. Similarly events that are no well, unpredictable, ambiguous and which occur at crucial moments would be perceived as more stressful than and event characterized by the opposite.

The second issue is related to how the person deals the situation once it has been perceived as being stressful, or the process of Secondary appraisal, which determines the nature off coping to be adopted. Two types of coping are possible: emotion focused coping or problem focused coping. The choice depends on the resources available to the person-health and energy resources, beliefs about control over the environment (about God or life in general), and problem solving skills, social skills and material resources. Certain personal constraints and environmental constraints may, however, mitigate the use of these coping resources. Personal constraints may be internalized values, while environmental constraints include demands that compete for the same resources.

The third issue focuses on the outcomes of stress. These refer to the pattern of reaction that defines the presence of stress. These may range from emotional experiences, motor manifestations, and alterations in adaptive functioning to physiological reactions. A combination of these is also possible. The exact nature of the reaction will depend on the nature of the secondary appraisal, or the particular coping strategy decided upon.

Systems Model of Stress

The Systems Model of Stress proposed by Lumsden (1975) attempts to take into consideration all the salient features of the different models, and calls for systems analysis of stress. As the name suggests, the emphasis is on the word 'system', which parts. The stress system is conceived of as an open system, which is continually interacting with the environment. The stress process is conceptualized as being dynamic and homeostatic in nature rather than a simple equilibrium model.

Sources of Stress

Generally it is believed that stress results from and imbalance between environmental demands and personal adequacies to meet those demands. However, management of stress is not possible unless the individual is aware of the specific sources of stress.

Stress can emanate from a variety of sources. Pestonjee (1992) has identified three important sectors of life from which stress may originate.

Jobs and Organisation:

These refer to the totality of the work environment, such as job description, work culture, interpersonal relationships and compensation offered.

Social Sector:

Denotes the socio cultural milieu of a person. It may include religion, caste, language, attitudes and beliefs of others, the political and legal environment etc.

Intrapsychic Sector:

This encompasses those aspects which are intimate and personal such as an individual's values, abilities, temperament, personality, needs, expectations and health.

This model further contends that each of these three sectors operate in a complex, interactive manner, rather than merely being summated together.

Proposing a somewhat different categorization, Brown (1984) has listed five categories.

Customary anticipated life events (any major change in life), such as marriage, divorce, beginning/ending of school, children leaving home and retirement.

Unexpected life events (any major life event which occurs suddenly), for example, unexpected bereavement, sudden loss of job, major accident, becoming aware of a terminal illness.

Progressive, accumulating situational events (any continuously recurring problems in life's activities) like daily hassles, job and family stress, school stress and competition.

Personality glitches (any personal traits that create social problems), such as poor communication, low self-esteem, insecurity, lack of confidence, poor decision-making and fear of failure.

Value dependent traits (circumstances generating thought-feeling conflict), for instance, revolutions, broken homes, moral dilemmas such as cheat or fail and peer pressure v/s personal conscience.

Stress at work

When we consider work stress in particular, research indicates six major sources of pressures (Cartwright and Cooper, 1997).

These are as follows:

1. Factor intrinsic to the job: These are related to poor working conditions, shift work, long hours, travel, risk and danger, poor technology, work under load and overload.

2. Role in the organization: When a person's role in the organization is clearly defined, stress can be kept to a minimum. Whereas Cartwright and Cooper mention only three aspects, Pareek (1993) has provided a fairly comprehensive list of stresses commonly encountered with reference to none's roe in the organisation.

3. Relationships at work: As early as in 1946, Selye had pointed out that 'good relationships between members of a group are a key factor in individual and organizational health'. There are three critical interpersonal relationships at work: relationships with one's boss, those with one's subordinates, and those with bone's colleagues.

4. Career development factor: Includes the degree of job security, fear of job loss, obsolescence of one's skills and capabilities and retirement. For many workers, career progression is of overriding importance. Performance appraisals (actual or even the fear of potential appraisal) can be an extremely stressful experience.

5. Organisational structure and climate: Non-participation at work and a general lack of control in the organisation re related to a variety of stress related symptoms.

6. Non-work pressures: Include pressures on the home front d8ue to job stress. Another commonly seen effect is that due to dual careers, especially for women. The dual career family model may be a source of stress for men as well. The amount of time they are able to devote to their jobs, the degree of mobility they have, the acceptance of transfers change if the wife is also working.

On the basis of above description, the generalize model of stress sources is presented showing following features

- Sources at Home
- Daily hassles of life
- Major life stresses
- Stress and the life cycle (adolescence, adulthood, old age)
- Relocation (due to man-made projects, natural calamities, bereavement of spouse, retirement, old age)
- Sources at work
- Daily hassles at work
- Organisational role stress
- Interpersonal relationships stress
- Career development associated stress
- Stress due to the organizational culture and climate

Since no individual is totally relegated to the home or the work sphere, the various sources interact with each other. This produces a third source of stress.

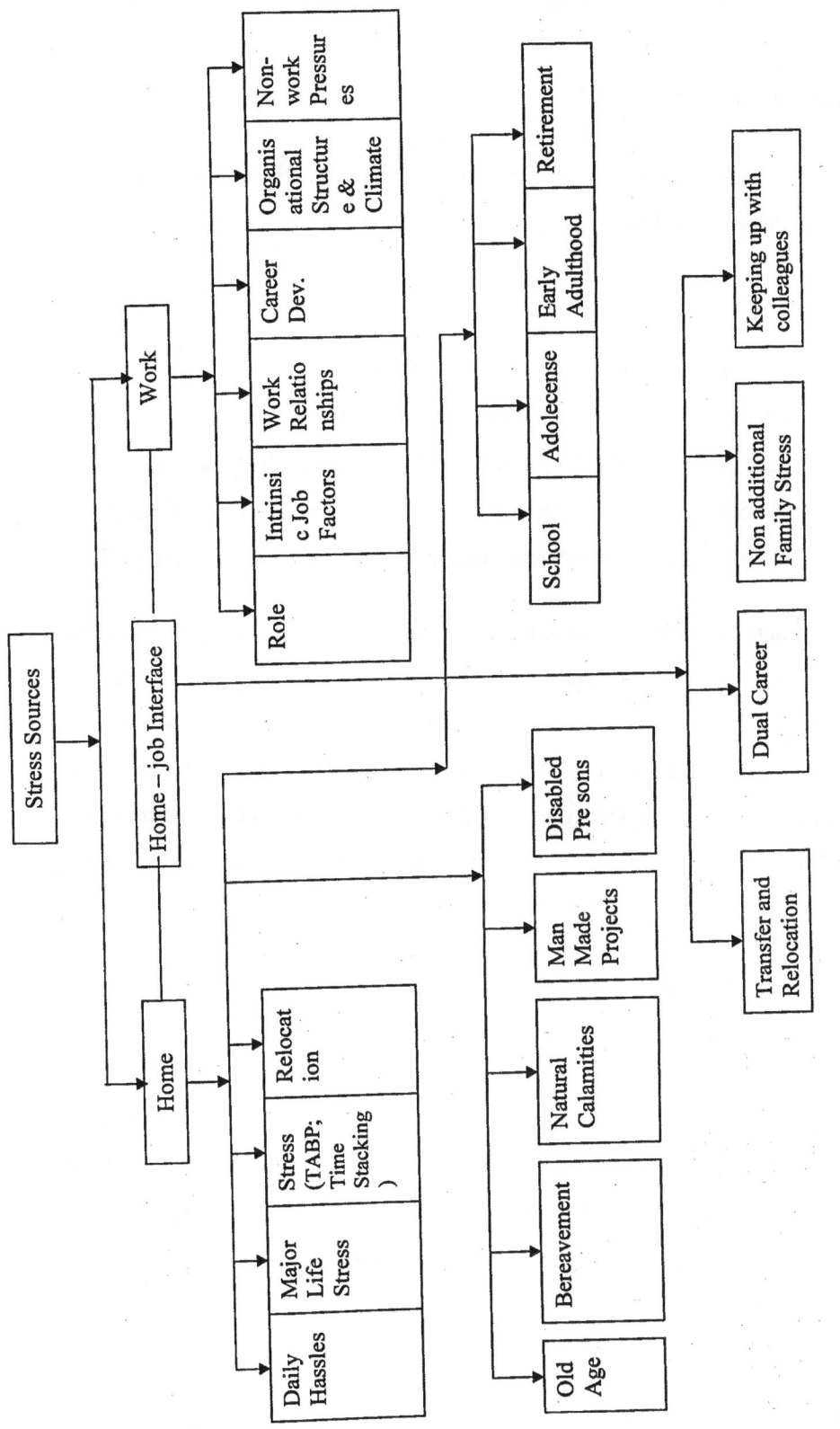

Figure 2 A Generalized Model of Stress Sources

Consequences of Stress

Most researchers and practitioners agree to the following four components of the consequences of the stress.

Physiological consequences

In order to prepare the person to cope with negative or positive environmental demands, certain 'automatic' physiological changes (governed by the autonomic nervous system) are triggered off. These changes help to raise body processes to the level required. Stress affects the heart rate, respiration, blood pressure and digestion, among others. Once the danger/emergency has passed, the system returns to normal.

A major physiological consequence is hypertension. What is hypertension? It is nothing but high blood pressure. Simply stated, blood pressure refers to the pressure of the heart that forces blood to various parts of the body. This pressure varies with the time of the day, adjusting to the demands of the body. It is generally lowest in the early hours of the morning when we are in deep sleep, and rises sharply when we get up, begin our day, or during exercise. Hypertension denotes the condition when the blood pressure is consistently higher than normal.

Among many reasons for hypertension is the lifestyle of the person. It has generally been observed that hypertensive persons have Type-A Behaviour Patterns, I.e., they are target-oriented, aggressive and cannot tolerate being looked down upon and, therefore, aim ever higher and higher. Their sympathetic nervous system remains in a constant state of heightened activation leading to thickening of the blood vessels or arteriosclerosis. Blood pressure is also affected by the emotional state of the person. Excitement, anger or tension can raise BP, but is comes down to normal within a couple of minutes.

Though hypertension may not be associated with any symptoms, yet it may kill a person slowly. Complications due to high BP include erosion of end organs such as the kidneys, heart, brain and eyes. It can lead to a hart attack, thickening of the heart muscles, heart failure or heart enlargement, stroke, cerebral haemorrhage, renal failure, poor vision, etc. A common misconception is that if a person's BP is high, he will suffer from giddiness. Most of the time, the symptoms are incidental.

The physiological consequences of stress are not limited to hypertension or cardiac conditions. Another major effect is on the immune system (Lovallo, 1997). Since Selye's work in 1936, we have come a long way in our understanding of the stress-health interface. Immunologists had earlier believed that the immune system is fairly autonomous in its functioning, responding only to the presence of illness. Recent findings reveal that the immune system is ultimately under behavioral control. (Felten et. al., 1991).

The Emotional Consequences

Emotions refer to the feeling aspect of behaviour such as mild irritation, rage, despair, sadness, love and liking. However, whereas the physiological effects of stress can be clearly pinpointed, observed and measured, emotional changes are highly subjective. One can experience them, but one cannot express them in words. Often a person may be seething with anger within, but maintains a cool exterior, clearly indicating that emotions are not always observable. In general, emotions are internal states, which are often short-lived, and can even be experienced in combination (one can feel anger, fear and even pleasure at the same time). Three identifiable emotional constellations that are a fairly regular outcome of stress are anxiety, anger and depression.

Anxiety: Generally an unpleasant emotional state accompanied by physiological arousal and cognitive aspects like apprehension, guilt and a sense of impending disaster. It is different from fear which is an emotional reaction to a specific or identifiable object.

Depression: A reaction characterized by apprehension, self-devaluation and feelings of guilt and worthlessness, dejection and a pervasive pessimistic outlook.

Anger: This is one of the offshoots of stress. It may be manifested in a variety of forms. We may express our anger, bottle it up, or distort it till it becomes something else.

Expressing anger may develop into a bad habit, leading to poor emotional control and unnecessary temper tantrums. It may grow out of proportion, be inappropriate to the situation and may sour many a relationship. It may also lead to strong feelings of guilt on one's part and retaliation from the person on whom the anger was vented.

Bottling up anger is another way. But this, too, may be unhealthy. It may cause somatic symptoms such as headaches, ulcers, bowel problems, skin problems, high blood pressure and heart attacks. Suppression of anger may also lead to self-hatred.

Neither untimely expression nor suppression provides the answer. It is not wrong to be angry. Anger can be a strong motivation. It is the force which makes us agitated when we are wronged. The problem is learning how to discharge our anger in a way which is not only acceptable to society but also healthy for us.

The Behavioral Consequences

Stress may do considerable damage to a person internally, but there are external manifestations too. The most important and probably the most relevant for the manager is how stress affects the ways in which people behave the effects on their interpersonal behaviour. There are at least three important areas of interpersonal behavior which are affected: relationships within the family, relationships with peers, and relationships with other people. We may dump our negative feelings, our frustrations, and our tensions on our family members or our friends (Who often have nothing to do with the cause of the stress). Some of the commonly seen behavioral effects are:

- Arguments and fights over relatively trivial matters.
- Overdependence.
- Uncommunicativeness.
- Unreasonableness.
- Withdrawal of love
- Lack of interest/over interest in sex.

The Cognitive Consequences

The relationship between stress and mental functioning is in the form of a U-shaped function. Thus, moderate levels of stress are considered optimal for mental operations such as attention, learning, problem solving and creativity. At lower levels of stress, one fails to be attentive enough (may show all the signs of boredom, weariness, lack of interest, lethargy), and at higher levels, cognition may become highly distorted. Some of the distortions are as follows:

- Greater attention paid to negative aspects of life and work.
- Inability to concentrate due to constant worry and anxiety.
- Overemphasis on self rather than on task.
- Problems in responsiveness to incidental data (e.g., one may focus just on the words used by the boss but not the context).
- Narrowing span of attention, i.e., the number of things or aspects that that one can attend to simultaneously.

An individual under stress may or may not manifest all these consequences. Cognitive analysis of stress clarify that the latter may be unique to the person, depending on the person's capacity for tolerance of cognitive and biologic demands, on the duration of the externally controlled stimulation, or on the capacity to control the duration of the stressors by coping and defensive cognitive processing.

The stressed person attempts to ward off the stressor, so as to restore balance. These attempts can be termed as coping. Of course, it is a different matter whether one's attempts are successful or not. Unsuccessful attempts at coping only cause greater disturbance, and like the proverbial violin string, eventually break the person.

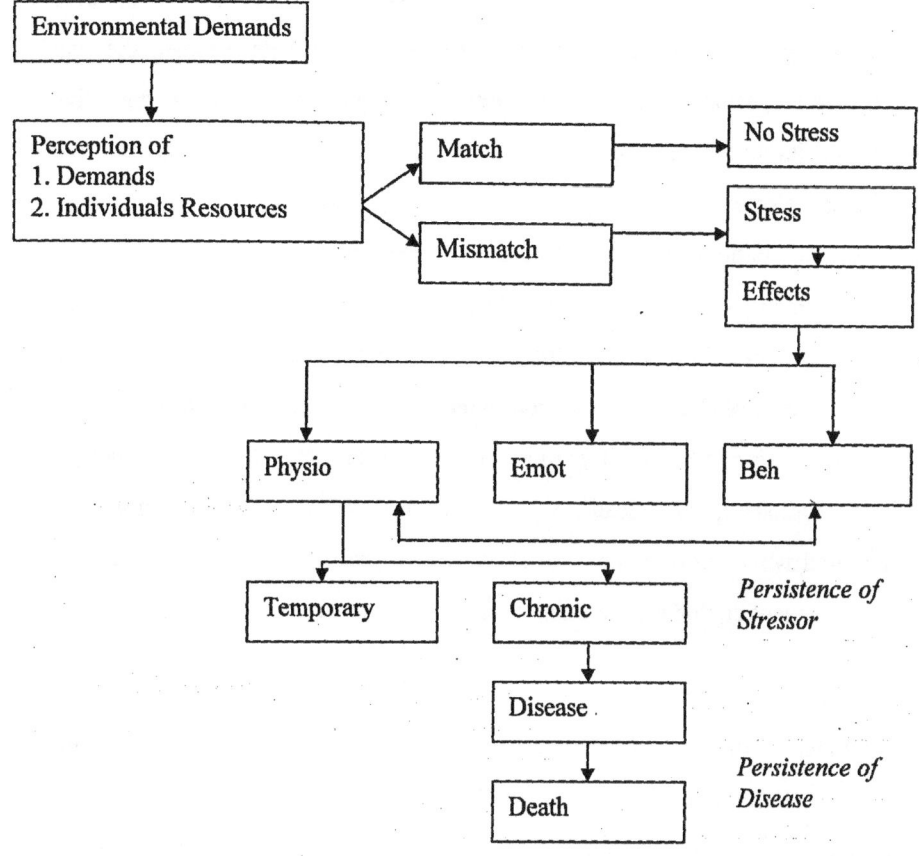

Figure 3 : Effects of Stress

Coping with stress:

The emotional and physical strain that accompanies stress is uncomfortable, people are motivated to do things to reduce their stress. These 'things' are what is involved in coping. Since stress involves a perceived discrepancy between the demands of the situation and the resources of person. Since people engage in coping in an effort to neutralize or reduce stress, coping activities are geared towards decreasing the person's appraisal of or concern for this discrepancy.

Coping can be understood as behavioural and cognitive efforts by the person to deal with both environmental and internal demands and conflicts between the two (Coyne and Holroyd, 1982). More so, it may be person's constantly changing cognitive behavioural efforts to manage specific external or/and internal demands that are appraised as taxing or exceeding the person's resources (Lazarus and Folkman, 1984a). The coping process is not a single event because coping involves ongoing transactions with the environment, the process is best viewed as a dynamic series of continuous appraisals and reappraisals of the shifting person - environment relationships. They may also be the result of changes in the environment that are independent of the person and his or her coping activity. Regardless of its source, any shift in the person environment relationship will lead to a re-evaluation of what is happening, its significance, and what can be done. The re-evaluation process or reappraisal, in turn influences subsequent coping efforts Lazarus and Folkman, (1984 b).

Thus coping is the process by which people try to manage the perceived discrepancy between the demands and resources they appraise in a stressful situation (Sarafino, 1990). The coping efforts can be quite varied and do not necessarily lead to a solution of the problem. Although coping efforts can and some would argue, should be aimed at correcting or mastering the problem, they may also simply help the person alter his or her perception of a discrepancy, tolerate or accept the harm or threat and escape or avoid the situation (Lazarus and Folkman, 1984b; Moos and Schaefer, 1986).

Functions of coping:

According to Lazarus (1987), coping can serve two main functions. It can alter the problem causing the stress or it can regulate the emotional response to the problem. Emotion focused coping is aimed at controlling the emotional response to the stressful situation. People can regulate their emotional response through behavioural and cognitive approaches. People tend to use emotion-focused approaches when they believe that they can do nothing to change the stressful situation. Problem focused coping is aimed at reducing the demands of stressful situations or expanding the resources to deal with it. People tend to use problem-focused approaches when they believe that their resources or demands of the situation are changeable.

Resource management process views the benefits of coping as gains in or savings of resources, whereas, the costs of coping incorporate allocation, loss and consumption of resources. An individual copes with stress by means of replacement, substitution or investment of resources (Hobfoll, 1989). Some particularly hardy individuals may be relatively immune to stressors that would impair most people's functioning (Kobasa, 1979). In general, increased level of stress threatens a person's well-being and produce automatic, persistent attempts to relieve the tension. Stress forces a person to do something, what is done depend on many influences. Sometimes inner factors such as a person's frame of reference, motives, competencies or stress tolerance play the dominant role in determining his or her coping strategies. At other times environmental conditions such as social demands and expectations are of primary importance. Any stress reaction, of course reflect the interplay of inner strategies and outer conditions some more influential than other, but all working together to make the person react in a certain way.

In reviewing certain general principles of coping with stress it is helpful to conceptualize three interactional levels. On a biological level there are immunological defenses and damage-repair mechanism, on a psychological and interpersonal level there are learned coping patterns, self defenses and support from family and friends, and on a sociocultural level there are group resources such as labours unions, religious organizations and law enforcement agencies. The failure of coping efforts on any of these levels may seriously increase a person's vulnerability on other levels.

Coping Styles:

What types of coping styles and strategies do people use in altering the problem or regulating their emotional response when they experience stress? Following sources suggest some commonly used methods:

Direct action: involves doing something specially and directly to cope with a stressor It includes problem focused coping, negotiating, consulting, arguing, punishing.

>Seeking information: involves acquiring knowledge about stressful situation knowledge that can then be used in promoting problem focused or emotion focused coping.

>Turning to others: The person seeks help, reassurance and comfort from family friends or other people.

>Resigned acceptance: The person comes to terms with problem situation and accepts it as it is. It is especially, suitable in emotion focused coping.

Emotional discharge is a method in which people express their feelings or reduce their tension when under stress. (Screaming, crying, using jokes)

Intrapsychic processes: uses cognitive strategies to reappraise a stressful situation. A wide variety of such strategies are used to regulate emotional reactions. (a) Cognitive redefinition: Try to put a good face on a bad situation. (b) Cognitive strategies: or defense mechanisms of Freud: which involve distorting memory or reality in some way. (c) Avoidance of problem and attention given to the problem.

Research has revealed two important patterns in the way people cope. First, individuals tend to be consistent in the way they cope with a particular type of stressor that is when faced with the same problem people tend to use the same methods they used in the past (Stone and Neale, 1984). Second, people seldom use just one method to cope with stressor. Their efforts typically involve a combination of strategies.

There are several ways in which people can help themselves and others cope with stress: social support, personal control and hardiness, organizing one's world better and time management, exercising to increase fitness, preparing for stressful events help in reducing the potential for stress.

Lazarus (1981), described four basic models of coping: Instrumental strategies or direct actions: are directed towards managing the threat or stressor itself.

Intrapsychic strategies are aimed primarily at regulating or minimizing the accompanying emotional distress. Inhibition of action: refers to the ability to resist taking action when such action would increase the likelihood of harm, danger or conflict with moral restraints. Information seeking: involves the instrumental activity of gaining a basis for action and also is a form of support mobilization that can relieve emotional distress.

Roger et. al. (1993) provided operational meaning of the four Types of coping styles.

Adaptive coping styles

Rational or Active coping means realistically accepting the stressful situation, without precluding the possibility of action. It is task oriented coping style with planning and rational thinking and represents adaptive coping style.

Detached coping feeling of detachment does not involve denial or attempt to avoid stress (Roger, 1992). Subjects reported that the 'less involved' they felt with the event the more effectively they were able to cope. Detachment could be distinguished from task-oriented strategies but detachment is considered to be adaptive coping style'.

Maladaptive coping styles

Avoidance coping is considered as helplessness. It includes behavioural disengagement or giving up. It also includes denial. It is a negative kind of behaviour involving withdrawl and giving up. Emotional coping involves expressing feelings and seeking emotional support.

EMOTIONAL CONTROL

Observations of human behaviour which resulted in the elaboration of the ancient Hippocrates-Galen typology led to the conclusion that individual differences in emotional reactions are one of the main components of the temperamental characteristics. The emotional mood, as well as emotional tone of behaviour, depends- according to Greek physicians on the predominance of one of the four 'Cardinal humours'.

Kant, referring to this ancient typology described in his Anthropology two of the four classic temperaments, the sanguine and the melancholic, entirely on the basis of emotional traits. Taking into account the temporal aspect and intensity of emotional reactions, Kant characterized sanguine as expressing strong emotions which proceed rapidly but superficially. On the other hand, the melancholic expresses deep rooted, slow arising and long lasting emotions.

Wundt (1911) stated that excitability is to sensory sensitivity as temperament is to emotions. This statement proposes that temperament is a predisposition to affective behaviour. Kretschmer (1944) considered mood, emotional tone (pleasure Vs unpleasantness) and emotional sensitivity as belonging to the main components of temperament. Heymans and Wiersma (1906-1909) considered three primary temperamental traits: activity, perserveration and emotionality. Emotionality is the frequency and intensity of emotional reactions in relation to situations by which they have been evoked. Emotionality refers to both positive and negative emotions. Allport (1937) is of the view that temperament refers to the characteristic phenomena of an individual's emotional nature, including his susceptibility to emotional stimulation, his customary strength and speed of response, the quality of his prevailing mood, and all peculiarities of fluctuation and intensity in mood, these phenomena being regarded as dependent upon constitutional make up and therefore largely hereditary in origin.

Eysenck (1970) stated that temperament being a part of the personality structure is a more or less stable and enduring system of affective behaviour (emotion). Goldsmith and Campos (1986) who specify the quality of emotions constituting temperament, conceive of temperament as individual differences in emotionality. This includes individual differences in the primary emotions fear, anger, sadness, pleasure, interest and more generalized arousal as expressed in temporal and intensive parameters of behavioral response.

The demarcated denominator of these statements is that temperament should be regarded as a construct referring exclusively to emotional behaviour. These definitions say that more or less stable individual differences in emotions are the subject of temperament research. Teplov (1985), Nebylitsyn (1976) and Merlin (1973) the leading researchers on temperament define this construct as referring to relatively stable individual differences in the dynamics of behaviour as determined by the type of nervous system. Nebylitsyn concludes that the structure of temperament consists of two basic traits: activity (motor behaviour) and emotionality. Emotionality embodies a large range of traits characterizing the rise, the course and the termination of the variety of affects, emotions and moods. Merlin mentioned emotional excitability, intensity of emotions and anxiety as emotional traits of temperament.

Strelau (1983), in his RTT considers temperament, manifested in the formal properties of reactions, revealing themselves in al kinds of behaviour, including emotional reactions. Emotional sensitivity belongs to the main characteristics of behavioral reactivity.

Thomas, Chess and Birtch (1968); and Thomas & Chess (1977) refer to biological, motor and emotional functions as dimensions of temperament. Closely related to emotional behaviour are the dimensions approach withdrawal, adaptability, intensity of reaction and quality of mood. A configuration of traits referring mainly to emotional characteristics constitute a factor labeled as factor A (so called difficult child).

Buss and Plonin (1984) also consider, structure of temperament to be composed of three primary dimensions: emotionality, activity and sociability. Emotionality consists of three basic emotional traits: distress, fear and anger. Rothbart and Derryberry (1981) consider self regulation component of temperament to be composed of attention, emotional and behavioural processes aimed at modulating the reactivity state of the organism. Emotionality is composed of negative emotionality (discomfort, fear, frustration sadness) and positive emotionality (pleasure and relief) – Derryberry and Rothbart (1984).

Thus the role of emotionality is of crucial importance in understanding temperament. In other words it can be illustrated that emotionality is inseparable component of temperament. The psychometric model of temperament introduced by Guilford et. al. (1976) also illustrates the significance of emotional trait. This is indicated by the fact that the only third order factor is emotional health (EH), which is composed of two second order factors emotional stability (E) and paranoid disposition (Pa), which in turn are composed of 13 first order temperamental traits.

The most general term which characterizes emotion as a trait is emotionality, which refers to individual differences in the formal characteristic of emotion (intensity, speed, changeability) and in the quality of emotions. Izard (1979) used the concept of emotion and affect interchangeably. Thus individual differences in affect can be considered under the term emotionality.

Six meanings of emotionality which refer to different phenomena in temperament research are:

(a) Emotionality as referring to personality traits based on the concept of optimal level of arousal:

Royce and Powell (1983) consider personality as being composed of six integrative systems: sensory, motor, cognition, affect, style and value. The affective system which transforms information in order to establish optimal levels of internal arousal suggest roughly speaking, the part of personality known as temperament. The structure of affective system, which is mainly presented from the point of view of individual differences approach, consists exclusively of configurations of traits and factors; thus it is possible to consider the affective system as a synonym for emotionality system. The factors of emotionality are emotional stability, emotional independence and introversion/ extraversion. There factors are regulated by specific arousal systems. Emotional stability by the limbic arousal; emotional independence by hormonal arousal and introversion extraversion by reticular arousal.

(b) Emotionality as individual difference in experience of arousal manifested in emotional states:

Thayer (1978), studying states of activation on the basis of verbal reports, was able to separate two independent dimensions of activation which refer to individual differences in arousal. Activation dimension A represents variation of the waking and sleeping cycle. On one pole it is characterized by experience of such psychological states as energetic, vigorous, lively, full of pep and active. The other pole includes sensations such as tired, sleepy, drowsy and wide awake. Activation dimension A refers to action oriented personality/ temperament dimensions. However, dimension B comprises the experience of arousal self reported in terms of emotional states. This dimension can be regarded as a synonym of emotionality. Thayer (1985) suggests that the physiological mechanism of activation dimension B may be in the limbic arousal system. High arousal of B factor is experienced as unpleasant emotional states related with tension and stress related arousal.

(c) Emotionality as individual differences in negative & positive emotions:

Goldsmith & Campos (1982, 1986) conceive emotionality both positive and negative emotions. Emotions constituting the structure of temperament comprise of anger, fear, sadness, distress, surprise, disgust, interest and joy. Existence of discrete emotion is universal.

(d) Emotionality as limited to negative emotions:

Buss and Plomin (1975, 1984) limit emotionality to negative emotions. Emotions include three components: expression, feeling and arousal. There is no agreement among researchers regarding classification of emotional expressions. It is impossible to study objectively the feeling (experiential) component of emotions. Thus arousal component is important. Emotions differ in the level of arousal involved.

(e) Emotionality as a synonym of neuroticism and anxiety:

On the basis of eleven instincts (primary emotions) distinguished by McDougal et. al. (1991) and Eysenck (1970) extracted three factors, the first of which was general emotionality also called emotional instability. Eysenck uses emotional instability for neuroticism. Gray (1981) is of the view that neuroticism seems to be a secondary consequence of the interaction between anxiety and impulsivity system, whereas emotionally stable individuals are low in both anxiety and impulsivity.

The concept of emotionality refers to different phenomena. This term is used in a very broad sense to characterize all personality dimensions that refer to the concept of arousal. The individual regulates the amount of stimulation by approaching or avoiding it in such a way as to ensure an optimal level of arousal, understood as a physiological correlate of behaviour. Gray (1982) believes that individuals differ in sensitivity to positive and negative stimuli being determined by individual differences in specific structures of the limbic system.

Emotional control is defined as the tendency to inhibit the expression of emotional responses. Many tools used earlier include Picture frustration study, Defense mechanism inventory MMPI subscale. An alternate approach to measure emotional control involves use of questionnaire e.g. hostility and directions of hostility questionnaire. A more generalized questionnaire measure of response style is repression sensitization scale derived from MMPI subscales and is intended to provide a broader index of emotional expressiveness. Emotional control is seen primarily as a cognitive strategy aimed at inhibiting the overt expression of emotional responses.

A number of researchers have suggested that continued rumination over emotional distress might contribute to delayed recovery Cameron and Meichenbaum (1982), Roger and Nesshoever (1987) and Roger and Najarian (1989)have given four empirically discriminable scales entitled rehearsal, emotional inhibition, aggression control, and benign control. Rehearsal measures the tendency to be pre occupied with emotional upset about the past or future event. Rehearsal provides a cognitive strategy for coping with negative self concept and feelings of being victimized. Rehearsal correlates significantly with EPQ-N. Rehearsal also correlates significantly but inversely with interpersonal sphere of control. Rehearsal was expected to maintain arousal by continued preoccupation with the emotional upset of the task and it was predicted that subjects who scored high on rehearsal would take significantly longer to recover. Rehearsal correlates significantly with physiological indices of stress including delayed heart rate recovery (Roger and Jamieson, 1988), elevated cortisol secretion (Roger 1988).

Emotional inhibition refers to inhibition of experienced emotion ;or bottling up or inhibiting the expression of experienced emotion .There are widely held intuitive notions about cultural differences in emotion, emotional expressivity and emotional control (Oatley and Jenkins .1996,Wierzbicka , 1994). Anger is seen as negative and inappropriate behaviour by Japanese subjects, it is valued as independent and self assertive behaviour in the west. Emotional inhibition correlates significantly but inversely with sociability. Aggression control and benign control correlate moderately and appear to form part of the extraversion constellation. Benign control correlates substantially with established measures of impulsiveness and aggression control relates to problems of anger management. Low scores on benign control indicate impulsiveness.

Temperament

In the individual differences approach represented by trait theories of personality, temperament is considered as one of the elements in the structure of personality. Trait psychologists differ in their views regarding the number and types of traits by which personality is defined and this is also true for the understanding of the notion of temperament. The increasing interest in research on temperament that can be observed in the last decade goes together with the growing variety of theories as well as methodological issues regarding temperament. A recent text on temperament (Angleitner and Ostendorf, 1994) exemplifies to some extent the spectrum of these diversities and richness of problem being discussed in the area of temperament. The questions addressed in various researches relate to the "concept of temperament" (e.g., Goldsmith et. al. 1987), 'the structure' (e.g., Angleitner, 1990), 'development aspect' (e.g., Thomas and Chess, 1977), 'biological bases' (Eysenck, 1970; Gray, 1964), 'methodological issues' (Angleitner and Riemann, 1990), and 'importance for practical applications' (Chess and Thomas, 1986; Strelau, 1983, 1988).

The history of temperament begins over two thousand years ago with the views of Greek physician Galen. His physiological theory assumed four types of temperaments in personality, each determined by an internal substance: 1. The sanguine person having an excess of blood tends to be lively and upbeat. 2. The phlegmatic person having an excess of phlegm, tends to be slow moving and controlled. 3. The melancholic person, having an excess of black bile, tends to worry and be sad. 4. The choleric person, having an excess of bile, tends to be excitable and prone to anger. Hippocrates and Galen (see Hutchins, 1952) introduced the idea that individual differences in temperament may be explained by means of biological mechanisms. This idea was further developed in empirical research; Heymans and Wiersma (1906-1909) studied the inheritance of temperamental traits. The term temperament became popular in the middle ages along with the doctrine of the four humours. It meant then and still means, a "constitution or habit of mind, especially, depending upon or connected with physical constitution" (Allport, 1937). According to Pavlov (1952) "temperament constitutes the most general characteristic of every man, the most general and most essential characteristic of his nervous system."

It is believed that temperament like intelligence and /or physique might be said to designate a class of raw material from which personality is fashioned. It refers to the chemical climate or internal weather in which personality evolves. The more anchored a disposition is in native constitutional soil, the more likely it is to be spoken of as temperament. Allport is of the view that in order to make needed advances in the study of temperament we require much more research in human genetics, biochemistry, neurology, endocrinology and physical anthropology. Since personality is largely conditioned by temperament, the precise source of temperament should be known. But, what does temperament include? No clear answer is possible. It seems probable that a primary factor relates to drive and vigour or its opposite apathy.

Temperament may be regarded as the characteristic phenomena of an individual's emotional nature, including his susceptibility to emotional stimulation, his customary strength and speed of response, the quality of his prevailing mood and all pecularities of fluctuation and intensity in mood, these phenomena being regarded as dependent upon constitutional make up, and therefore, largely hereditary in orgin (Allport, 1961). Like physique and intelligence temperament may be altered, within limits by medical and nutritional influences, as well as in the course of learning and life experiences. A number of workers have made satisfied use of the four temperaments, among these are Galen, Kant, Wundt, Hoffding, Herbart and Pavlov.

Diamond, (1957) published his evolutionary approach to temperament. He described four temperaments shared by primates including man and some social mammals: fearfulness, aggressiveness, affiliated-ness and impulsiveness. He conducted no human research, nor did he offer specific means of testing his hypotheses.

Buss and Plomin, (1975) see temperaments as a subclass of personality traits, shared by our species and primates, and defined as being inherited and appearing early in life. To be more precise, "Temperament are inherited personality traits that appear during the first two years of life and endure as basic components of personality", Buss, and Plomin (1984). There are three defining properties of temperaments: (a) they are inherited (b) they appear early and (c) they endure. In contrast, there are personality traits that appear during infancy, but they are not inherited. There certainly are inherited personality traits that appear later in life. The four temperaments given by Buss and Plomin, (1975) are emotionality, activity, sociability and impulsivity, which are represented by the acronym EASI. Thus temperaments appear to be consistent with other inherited human psychological tendencies in being broad rather than narrow.

At the turn of the century Russian physiologist, Ivan Petrovich Pavlov (1951-1952) while studying conditioned reflexes in dogs arrived at the conclusion that individual differences in the speed and efficiency of conditioning as well as in the dog's behaviour in laboratory conditions can be explained by certain properties of the central nervous systems, (CNS). In the course of his work he developed a theory of nervous system processes that greatly amplified the classical theory of temperament. Pavlov postulated two extreme types of nervous system and two balanced types. The central nervous system properties as proposed by Pavlov include strength of excitation, strength of inhibition, the equilibrium of nervous processes and their mobility. Depending on the configuration of these properties, different types of Central Nervous System (CNS) may be distinguished. Pavlov being under the influence of the ancient

Greek temperament typology limited the number of CNS types to four. Basically he conceived of the types of CNS as the physiological basis of temperament. However, he used the terms types of nervous system (TNS) and types of temperament interchangeably, especially, when referring to nervous system types in humans. Thus the mentioned types are what we call in man temperaments.

Pavlov's theory of the types of CNS introduced in the first quarter of our century gained popularity, in the last quarter, especially, among the personality researchers with biological orientation (e.g., Bauchsbaum, 1978; Claridge, 1985; Eysenck, 1972; Strelau, 1983; and Zuckerman, 1979). The reason for renewed interest in properties of CNS may be explained by at least two facts. First, Pavlov's typology offers the most adequate physiological interpretation of temperament that's why it is still popular among laymen and professionals. Second, the Pavlovian constructs of strength of CNS and of protective inhibition are closely related to the concept of arousal (activation) to which most biologically oriented personality theories refer (e.g., Strelau and Eysenck, 1987).

Pavlovian CNS properties:

Pavlov (1951-52), while defining the basic CNS properties did not refer to physiological mechanisms as the names of these properties suggest. He characterized them from functional point of view, stressing the role they play in the process of individual's adaptation to the environment. Thus he took behaviouristic position in defining and studying all the four CNS properties, which he regarded, when referring to man as temperamental characteristics.

(a) Strength of nervous system as excitation (Endurance):

Pavlov defined strength of excitation as the functional capacity of the nervous system, thus the ability of the cortical cells to work. This property may be defined as endurance of the CNS in face of continuous excitation. Situations, settings, tasks and certain stimuli characteristic like degree of variation, novelty, intensity, complexity and meaningfulness etc. may be the sources of stimulation. Individuals in whom transmarginal inhibition occurs in reaction to stimuli of low intensity or duration are characterized as having a weak CNS; whereas, individuals with a strong CNS are able to react adequately to stimuli of high intensity and long duration. The strong type has a higher endurance or working capacity.

(b) Strength of nervous system as inhibition:

Strength of inhibition refers to conditioned inhibition i.e., ability to maintain a state of conditioned inhibition, such as extinction differentiation delay and conditioned inhibition in its narrow meaning. Individuals with weak nervous system or with weak inhibitory processes are unable to sustain conditioned inhibition for long time. In individuals having strong inhibitory process prolonged conditioned inhibition does not cause disturbance.

(c) Equilibrium of nervous system:

The equilibrium of nervous system should be regarded as the ratio of the strength of excitation and strength of inhibition. The functional meaning of this property consists of the ability to inhibit certain excitation, when required in order to evoke other reactions in combination with the environmental demands.

(d) Mobility of nervous processes:

Pavlov (1951-52) has defined Mobility of nervous processes as the ability of CNS to respond adequately as soon as possible to continuous changes in the environment. It manifests itself in the ability to react quickly and adequately to changes in the surroundings. The essence of mobility is the ability to give way according to external condition to give priority to one impulse before the other, on fore inhibition and conversely (Pavlov 1951-52).
51-52).

Pavlovian CNS Properties and Temperament:

In his description of the properties of nervous system, Pavlov maintained that his four types of nervous system (TNS) correspond to the classical four types of temperament as defined by Hippocrates and Galen: (a) Sanguine - strong, balanced excited. (b) Phlegmatic-strong, balanced, inhibited. (c) Melancholic - weak, unbalanced inhibited. (d) Choleric- strong, unbalanced, excited.

According to the prevailing opinion it is said that the innate type of central nervous system constitute the physiological basis of temperament. Different configurations of the three properties of strength, mobility and balance constitute the four types of nervous system distinguished by Pavlov, namely, (a) weak type (b) strong and unbalanced type (c) strong balanced and slow type (d) strong balanced and mobile type (Strelau 1983).

The founders of Neo-Pavlovian Typology:

Since the mid fifties the Pavlovian typology gained popularity among Soviet psychologists and psycho-physiologists working with man, especially, with adult people. Two centers in which studies have been conducted in this field developed almost parallel – one in Moscow, headed by B.M. Teplov and the other one chaired by V.S Merlin, in Perm (so called Ural group). New facts and interpretations introduced by these researchers to Pavlov's typology caused a further development of this theory, calling it neo-Pavlovian typology.

The Teplov Nebylitsyn School:

There is no doubt that Teplov and his students, among whom V.D. Nebylitsyn hold an outstanding position, working with man and especially, with adults, have made the largest contribution to Pavlov's typology. Theoretical considerations and new evidence collected by them during the last quarter of our century brought revolutionary changes in the traditional typoloy of nervous system. Therefore the label neo-Pavlovian typology is fully justified. Gray (1964), Mangan (1982), Nebylitsyn (1972), Nebylitsyn and Gray (1972b), Strelau (1983), and Teplov (1964) have systematically explored the field.

(a) The strength of nervous system, understood by Pavlov as endurance of nervous system (NS) has been conceptualized by Teplov and Nebylitsyn (1963 b) as a bipolar dimension with endurance and sensory sensitivity as its two extremes. The ratio between these two factors being approximately constant.

(b) The mobility of NS has been split into two independent factors: mobility in its narrow sense, speed of alteration of the signal value of a pair of stimuli, and lability, which reveals itself in speed with which nervous processes are initiated and terminated (Teplov and Nebylitsyn, 1963 a).

(c) The dynamism has been identified as a new property of the NS. It is speed and facility with which the processes of excitation and inhibition are generated during the formation of conditioned responses (Nebylitsyn, 1972 a).

(d) The balance of nervous system has been conceived as a secondary property. It comprises strength, mobility, lability and dynamism in regard with excitation and inhibition (Nebylitsyn, 1972 a).

(e) Nervous system properties are regarded not only as the physiological basis of temperament as has been affirmed by Pavlov, but also as physiological mechanisms underlying aptitudes and general abilities (Nebylytsyn and Gray, 1972 b; Rusalov, 1979; Golubeva, 1980; and Leites, 1972).

The Ural Group: search for links between TNS and Temperament:

The contribution of V.S.Merlin and his students from Perm is practically unknown in the west, due to the fact that almost all of their publications appeared only in Russian. It was Merlin's group who paid considerable attention to the relation between NSPs and temperamental traits providing a bridge between Pavlov's typology and psychology. There exist a tremendous number of studies conducted by Merlin's students which show the significance of NS properties especially, the strength of the NS in the efficiency of performance in different life situations, including school performance (Utkina, 1964), sports (Vyatkin, 1978) and professional work (Strelau, 1985; Kopytowa, 1964). The general conclusion derived from the data collected in these studies is that in situations characterized as stimulation overload individuals with strong TNS perform better than individuals with weak TNS. This difference disappears however, when the stimulative value of the situation decreases.

From literature, it is evident that Pavlov's theory has undergone several stages of evolution. There exist different interpretations of this typology. This statement is true not only in relation to western interpreters of Pavlov's theory. Exactly the same applies, however, to Teplov, Nebylitsyn, Merlin and other researchers involved in Pavlovian Typology.

Regulative Theory of Temperament:

The Polish psychologist Jan Strelau (1983, 2001) has used Pavlov's theory as a springboard for his own conception. His major concepts are energetic level and temporal characteristics, which fully surfaced in his Regulative Theory of Temperament (RTT). According to regulative theory of temperament, temperament is relatively stable characteristic of behaviour. This means, among other things, temperamental traits are more stable or less prone to undergo changes than other behaviour characteristics.

The regulative theory of temperament (RTT) implies that temperament is above all a result of biological evolution (Strelau, 1983, 1987). The interpretation of this general statement says that: (1) Primarily temperament has a biological basis, (2) temperamental traits are present in the individual right from early childhood, (3) temperamental characteristics may be found not only in humans but also in animals, and (4) temperament refers first of all to the formal characteristics and not to the content of behaviour. Like Pavlov, Strelau (1983), considered that temperament is determined by an individual specific configuration of neurological and endocrine mechanisms regulating the level of arousal. If so, one of the consequences of the assumption that temperament has a biological background is that temperament is already present in early infancy. Researches of American temperament experts support this view (Bates, 1987; Buss and Plomin, 1975, 1984; Matheny et al. 1985; Ross, 1987).

Phenomenon of temperament is expressed in formal characteristics of behaviour having energetic and temporal features. These formal characteristics are present in all kinds of reaction and behaviour. "In Strelau's regulative theory of temperament, the temperament is defined as a set of relatively stable features of the organism that reveal themselves in such formal traits of behaviour as energetic level and temporal characteristics. Being primarily determined by inborn physiological mechanisms, temperament is subjected to slow changes caused by maturation and by some environmental factors" (Strelau, 1989).

Regarding structure of temperament: those traits should be included in the structure of temperament that refers to the formal aspect of behaviour expressed in energetic and temporal characteristics. In the RTT the structure of temperament comprises eight traits, two of which belong to energetic characteristics of behaviour: reactivity and activity and six to the temporal features: persistence, recurrence, mobility, regularity, speed and tempo. Much attention has been paid in RTT to traits referring to the energetic components of behaviour, which are significant for human adaptation, especially, in situations and for actions characterized by extreme stimulation.

Reactivity reveals itself in the intensity (magnitude) of reactions to acting stimuli. This temperamental trait co-determines the individual's sensitivity (sensory and emotional) and endurance (capacity to work). Endurance expresses itself in the ability to react adequately to strong and/or long lasting stimulation. Reactivity resembles the

Pavlovian concept of strength of excitation. In Gray's (1964), terminology, the high reactive individuals are characterized by high arousability.

Activity The second energetic characteristic of behaviour, in RTT is activity. Activity is a temperamental trait, which reveals itself in the amount and range of undertaken action (goal directed behaviour) of a given simulative value (Strelau, 1989). By means of activity the individual regulates, the stimulative value of behaviour and/or situations in such a way as to satisfy his or her need for stimulation (Eliasz, 1985; Strelau, 1983). The stimulative value of activity consists of the fact that activity by itself is a source of stimulation. The more complex and difficult the activity, the higher the stimulation being generated. Highly reactive individuals are low in activity, vice-versa low reactive individuals are high on activity.

Factor analysis of the six temperamental traits referring to the temporal characteristics of behaviour has shown that they can be grouped into two factors (Gorynska and Strelau, 1979).

Persistence Factor I has highest loading in persistence and recurrence of reaction. Since both traits refer to a kind of rigidity in behaviour, this factor may be identified as perseverance. It is similar to Heymans and Wiersma's (1906-1909) secondary function, also known as preservation and treated in terms of durability of reactions.

Tempo and speed have the highest loading for factor II. In the RTT, tempo is expressed in the number of homogeneous reactions performed in a given period of time, whereas, speed is defined by time required to generate reactions to given stimuli or situations (Gorynska and Strelau, 1979). Taking these characteristics into account factor II is labeled as liveliness.

Mobility, that is ability to switch behaviour in response to changes in the surroundings, shares its loading with both factor I and II. This suggests that mobility of behaviour is a secondary trait.

Modified RTT and meaning of Temperament. :

After reviewing the literature on temperament which was published in last few decades Strelau (1992, 1993) arrived at the conclusion that formal characteristics of behaviour are the most often met common denominator by means of which the nature of temperament has been described.

From the statement that temperament refers to formal characteristics of behaviour, following postulates may be formulated (Strelau and Zawadzki, 1993).

There exist relatively stable individual differences, with respect to the formal characteristics of behaviour encompassed by two basic categories intensity (energetic aspect of behaviour) and time (temporal aspect of behaviour).

Every behaviour, whatever its kind and content, can be characterized by means of energetic and temporal characteristics. Therefore, temperament may be expressed in all kinds of behaviour and reactions.

From early infancy, children differ in the intensity and temporal characteristics of their basic drives, reactions and behaviours, which means that from the beginning of postnatal life they may be characterized in terms of temperamental traits.

Whatever the specific behaviours typical of man and animals, all mammals (atleast) may be characterized by means of properties which refer to the categories of intensity and time, thus, temperament occurs in both humans and animals.

Taking into account postulate (3) and (4) it is reasonable to assume that temperament characteristics as expressed in early stages of development are mainly a product of biological evolution and that there must exist some genetic bases as well as physiological mechanisms co-determining individual differences in temperament.

Considering the postulates formulated above as well as the theoretical considerations on temperament to be met in literature, temperament may be defined in the following way: "Temperament refers to basic, relatively stable personality trait which apply mainly to formal aspects of reactions and behaviour" (energetic and temporal characteristics). These traits are present since early child hood and they occur in man and animals. Being primarily determined by inborn physiological mechanisms, temperament is subject to changes caused by maturation and by some environmental factors (Strelau, 1993).

Measurement of temperament and formal characteristics of behaviour:

Since the roots of RTT can be found, among other theories in the Pavlovian approach, the main inventory by means of which data referring to RTT were collected by Strelau and his coworkers was the Strelau Temperament Inventory (Strelau, 1972, 1983; Strelau, Angleitner, Bantelmann and Ruch, 1990). However, the STI (and the STI-R as well), measuring the Pavlovian constructs of strength of excitation, strength of inhibition and mobility of nervous processes does not grasp all traits postulated by RTT. For activity and temporal characteristics different inventories had to be developed. Such a state of affairs regarding the status of RTT has forced authors of RTT to develop an inventory, which correspond fully to theory under discussion. Its label: The Formal Characteristics of Behaviour Temperament Inventory (FCB-T1) underlies the fact that temperament as understood by Strelau refers not to content but to formal aspects of behaviour. The postulated structure and critical remarks based on theoretical considerations and empirical evidence were important for constructing the new inventory (Jan Strelau and Bogdan Zawadzki, 1993).

The characteristics measured by FCB-TI are given below:

Briskness (BR): tendency to react quickly, to keep a high tempo of performing activities, and to shift easily in response to changes in the surroundings from one behaviour reaction to another.

Perseverance (PE): tendency to continue and to repeat behaviour after cessation of stimuli (situations) evoking this behaviour.

Sensory sensitivity (SS): ability to react to sensory stimuli of low stimulative value.

Emotional Reactivity (ER): tendency to react intensively to emotion generating stimuli expressed in high emotional sensitivity and in low emotional endurance.

Endurance (EN): ability to react adequately in situations demanding long lasting or high stimulative activity and under intense external stimulation.

Activity (ACI): tendency to undertake behaviour of high stimulative value or to supply by means of behaviour strong stimulation from the surrounding.

The FCB-TI validity studies on Polish subjects by Jan Strelau and Bogdan Zawadzki, 1995 and FCB-TI, preliminary results of the Italian version by (Vilfredo De Pascalis, Bogdan Zawadzki and Jan Strelau, 2000) show nearly parallel results, proving that the test has cross-cultural applicability and that temperamental traits are nearly similar across different cultures.

Type-A Behaviour Pattern:

Cardiologists Meyer Friedman and Ray Rosenman while studying dietary differences in cholesterol intake between male heart disease victims and their wives discovered Type-A behaviour pattern. These researchers began to study this possibility by looking at differences between heart disease patients and similar people who were healthy, focusing on the subject's stress related behavioural characteristics. This comparison revealed differences in behavioural and emotional style: the patients were more likely than the non-patients to display a pattern of behaviour we now refer to as Type-A.

Type-A behaviour pattern is a particular action emotion complex which is exhibited by those individuals who are engaged in a relatively chronic struggle to obtain an unlimited number of poorly defined things from their environment in a shortest period of time and if necessary against the opposing efforts of other persons or things. Even though Friedman and Rosenman (1958), originally conceived of Type-A in terms of a person's interaction with the environment a tendency to behave in hostile, competitive and time urgent ways when confronted by challenge. Thoresen and Powell (1992), pointed out that most research has taken an overly simplistic approach, neglecting the kind of complex reciprocal interactions that are part of everyday life, example, a Type-A person is sensitive to threats of self esteem, may react with hostility to implied criticism from others, which may then offend others and help create the very kind of social environment the person is uncomfortable in (Smith and Anderson, 1985). In contrast low levels of competitiveness, time urgency and hostility characterize Type-B Behaviour Pattern. People with Type-B pattern tend to be more easygoing and philosophical about life, they are more likely to 'stop and smell the roses.

Friedman and Rosenman (1974), argued that Type-B individuals may be equally or even more ambitious than Type-A, but ambition associated with Type-B is characterized by confidence and satisfaction, whereas, ambition associated with Type-A behaviour pattern is dominated by anger and anxiety. Thus the nature of different traits associated with Type-A behaviour pattern predisposes a person towards the perception and experience of stress at work.

Friedman and Rosenman (1974), Chesney, Frautschi, and Rosenman (1985) have described three basic characteristics of TABP.

Competitive achievement orientation: Type-A individuals tend to be very self-critical and strive towards goals without feeling a sense of joy in their efforts or accomplishments.

Time urgency: Type-A people seem to be in a constant struggle against the clock. Often, they quickly become impatient with delays and unproductive time schedule commitments too tightly, and try to do more than one thing at a time, such as reading while eating or watching television.

Anger and Hostility: Type-A individuals tend to be easily aroused to anger or hostility, which they may or may not express overtly.

Research has confirmed that there are clearly observable differences between Type-A and Type-B individuals (for example Glass, 1977; Lovallo and Pishkin, 1980). In the presence of others, Type-A people become more competitive and achieve more, whereas, Type-B people show only small changes in performance (Suls and Sanders, 1988). People with Type-B pattern are less competitive, more patient and easygoing and tolerant and moved and talked more slowly, they were also less likely to suffer from a cardiovascular disease.

When challenged, Type-A individuals show more physiological arousal than Type-B Individuals (Dembroski and Mc Dougall, 1978; Strelau 2001) and exhibit an exaggerated need for achievement (Burnam, Pennebaker and Glass 1975). Thus heightened need for achievement is an important characteristic of people who exhibit Type-A coronary prone behaviour. Associated closely with need to achieve are attempts to avoid failure (Birney, Burdick and Teevan, 1969). Type-A individuals have been shown to have a distinct fear of failure (Gastorf and Teevan, 1980). Given their high need for achievement, it is not surprising that such people exhibit Type-A behaviours even in young age. Even in young children if mothers respond neutrally to achieving behaviours and punished unsatisfactory ones, her child is likely to develop a negative attitude towards achievement and to become motivated by a fear of failure (Teevan and McGhee, 1972). Matthews and Angulo (1980), assessed children's competitiveness, impatience and aggression. As might be expected children who could be classified as Type-A were more competitive, impatient and aggressive than Type-B children.

The development of a Type-A behaviour pattern can probably be traced to childhood relationships with parents and peers. From the existence of such behaviour patterns psychologists can infer a great deal about individual's motivation and how they will respond to various situations for coping. Type-A people have an intense desire to control their environment (Carver and Glass, 1978) and become irritated when others slow down their rapid pace (Glass, Synder and Hollis, 1974). Having one's behaviour blocked generally results in strong emotional responses and stress. House et al. (1982), suggest that central trait of Type-A is his desire for social achievement (reflected in ambition, competitiveness, aggressiveness etc.). This trait is analogous to extrinsic motivation for working (i.e., desire for money, status, recognition), which contribute strongly to perception and experience of stress at work place.

Glass (1977), proposes that Type-A individuals are more motivated than Type-B individuals to gain and maintain control over important environmental events, thus are more threatened by potential loss of control over stressful events than are Type-B individuals. Type-A individuals will:

- Work assiduously on a task whether instructions require such performance.
- Supers fatigue and other symptoms that might threaten there best efforts.
- Perform better than Type-B, after preexposure to uncontrollable and moderate stress.

Type-A behaviour pattern as a challenge and demand engendering style: Cognitive social learing theory (Bandura, 1977). Emerging cognitive approach to personality (Cantor and Kihlstrom, 1982) and interaction models of personality (Magnuson and Endler, 1977) provide a framework for examining such reciprocal relation between persons and situations. Type-A persons in contrast to Type-B persons construct a subjectively and objectively demanding and challenging environment in principally five ways.

- They choose to enter more objectively challenging and demanding situations.
- They appraise a given situation as involving more challenge or demand.
- Their cognitive coping behaviour during task performance serves as prolonged contact with stress.
- Their expression of Type-behaviour (for example hostility and competitiveness) elicits challenging or demanding behaviour from other individuals.
- They selectively attend feedback and evaluate their accomplishment in such a way as to retrospectively and generate a more negative view of their performance and increase the perceived need for further aggressive striving.

A number expert agrees that Type-A construct is quite useful. Thoresen and Powell (1992) recently analysed conceptual as well as empirical issues in Type-A theory and research and concluded that there is much potentially important work to be done with the construct, provided more careful attention is said to its interactional, cognitive and cultural aspects.

The characteristics of people possessing Type-A and Type-B behaviour patterns are tabulated below:

Characteristics of Type-A and Type-B Behaviour Pattern

	Type-A	Type-B
Speech	Loud, rapid, single word answers, immediate answer, sentences short and to the point, interrupt others, uses obscenities.	Soft, slows, measured answers with frequent pauses, pauses before answers, sentence long and rambling, rarely interrupts, rarely uses obscenities
Motor behaviour	Tense, alert, harsh laughter, on the edge of chair, smiles with side of mouth.	Relaxed, Calm, Gentle, chuckle, quiet, attentiveness, and broad smiles.
Attitudes and emotions	Competitive, wants to move up in the job, hate delays, humourless, ambitious, hostile.	Cooperative, satisfied with the job, does not delays, good sense of humour, unambiguous, friendly

Source: Chesney Eagleston and Rosenman (1980).

Type-A behaviour pattern and reaction to stress :

People with Type-A and Type-B behaviour pattern differ in the aspect of reaction to stress. In particular, recent evidence suggests that A's are more likely to give up and feel helpless, when confronted with certain types of stress than B's. And this in turn may lead them to demonstrate poorer and less adaptive behaviour strategies than B's. Direct evidence for the presence of such differences has recently been reported by Matthews (1982). Individuals were asked to work upon several simple problems of different shapes and sizes. Results suggest that Type-A persons react more strongly to stress than Type-B. As a result they may often seriously damage their own health. Further when they encounter stress, Type-A's seem to respond less adaptively to it. And then to make matters worse they often blame themselves even for negative outcomes they have not produced. Type-B's in contrast react with more effective behaviour strategies and show less tendency to shoulder blame or responsibility that is not really theirs.

Given these differences it is little wonder that relatively few top level managers are Type-As. On one hand they do not often survive long enough to rise to the highest ranks, on the other if they do, they fail to handle as well, as B's. This is not to say that Type-A's are always at a disadvantage. Competitiveness and achievement striving do often yield positive results. But, at last it appears that Type-A person should devote careful attention to techniques for coping with stress. If they do, the careers and the lives they save may well be their own.

Rationale of the present study:

Review of the related literature demonstrates that most of researches on stress have focused on the role of stimulus intensity and the sources of stress. Whereas, recent theoretical Interpretations lead to the fact that the actual state of stress is caused by the lack of equilibrium between demands and the capability of the individuals to cope with them. The capacity of the individual to cope with demands depend upon several psychological predispositions. The temperament / personality play crucial role in this setup. However, some studies have been conducted to examine the role of temperament risk factor in stress and emotion with a few temperamental traits and that too not having much conclusive findings.

Further Type-A behaviour pattern has its own functional effect on stress coping style and emotional control as well as goes with temperament traits known as formal characteristics of behavior. This may also influence relation between stress, coping styles, emotional control and temperamental traits.

Therefore keeping in view the potential relevance of the proposal discussed above the present study is proposed to examine the functional relationship between stress, coping styles and emotional control with temperament and Type-A behaviour pattern. Thus the problem of study can be stated as:

STRESS, COPING STYLES AND EMOTIONAL CONTROL AS A FUNCTION OF TEMPERAMENT AMONG TYPE - A INDIVIDUALS

The Main objectives of the study are as under

1. To examine the relationship between stress and temperamental traits.

2. To examine the relationship between coping styles and temperamental traits.

3. To examine the relationship between emotional control and temperamental traits.

4. To examine the differences in the relationship between stress and temperamental traits among Type-A, Type-AB and Type-B individuals.

5. To examine the differences in the relationship between coping styles and temperamental traits among Type-A, Type-AB and Type-B individuals.

6. To examine the differences in the relationship between emotional control and temperamental traits among Type-A, Type-AB and Type-B individuals.

7. To examine the differences in the relationship between stress and coping styles among Type-A, Type-AB and Type-B individuals.

8. To examine the differences in the relationship between stress and emotional control among Type-A, Type-AB and Type-B individuals.

9. To examine the differences in the relationship between coping styles and emotional control among Type-A, Type-AB and Type-B individuals.

10. To discover the overlapping factors among the measures of stress, coping style, emotional control and temperamental traits.

Specific Hypotheses:

In the light of theoretical conceptualizations in related areas and earlier researches in the field, following hypotheses have been proposed:

1. Stress correlates significantly with temperamental traits.

2. Coping styles correlate significantly with temperamental traits.

3. Emotional control correlates significantly with temperamental traits.

4. The relationship between stress and temperamental traits differ among Type-A Type-AB and Type-B individuals.

5. The relationship between coping styles and temperamental traits differ among Type-A, Type-AB and Type-B individuals

6. The relationship between emotional control and temperamental traits differ among Type-A, Type-AB and Type-B individuals.

7. Relationship between stress and coping styles differs among Type-A, Type-AB and Type-B individuals.

8. Relationship between stress and emotional control differs among Type-A, Type-AB and Type-B individuals.

9. Relationship between coping styles and emotional control differs among Type-A, Type-AB and Type-B individuals.

10. Stress, coping styles, emotional control and temperamental traits shall have overlapping factor structure.

11. The factor structure of the measures differs among Type-A, Type-AB and Type-B individuals.

CHAPTER – II

REVIEW OF LITERATURE

REVIEW OF LITERATURE

For the present investigation the review of related literature being large is presented under six headings.

1. Stress and Temperament: In a recent review of studies on relationship between stress and temperament, Strelau (1995, 2001) accepts that it should be considered a starting point for formulating hypotheses regarding some aspects of the stress temperament relationship. He further views that temperament is one of the many personal variables that cannot be ignored for a proper understanding of human functioning under stress including community stress, especially, when analyzing behaviour disturbances resulting from excessive or chronic states of stress.

It is well known that excessive or chronic stress leads to behaviour disorders, maladaptive functioning and pathology. The studies conducted by Thomas and Chess (1977), and Thomas et. al. (1968), should be regarded as pioneer work which has shown that behaviour disorders in children cannot be explained by the unfavourable environmental factors only and that an essential part of the variance in behaviour disorders refers to a given configuration of temperamental traits called by them 'difficult temperament'. The pattern of difficult temperament comprises such categories as irregularity, slow adaptability to changes in environment, intense negative mood and withdrawl responses to new situations or strange persons.

Studies conducted by Maziade and co-workers (1989, 1990) in the domain of psychiatric disorders have shown that extreme temperaments in terms of easy and difficult temperament, when taken alone are bad predictors of clinical outcome. However, when these temperament constellations are considered in interaction with stressors, consisting in these studies of family dysfunctional behaviour control, they became essential predictors of psychiatric disorders. This finding was replicated in several longitudinal studies at different ages.

Aldwin et. al. (1989) conducted a study on over one thousand adult men to show the effect of one temperament trait, emotionality, in moderating the effect of stressors on the vulnerability to behaviour disorders. This study showed that individuals characterized by high emotionality report more stressors as compared with low emotional persons. Using multivariate analysis of data the authors have shown that emotionality had a stronger effect on mental health than hassles and life events, but that together, emotionality, life events and hassles accounted for almost 40% of the variance in mental health symptoms.

The data reported by Maziade et. al. (1990), showed that there was no statistically significant difference between extreme temperament at age seven and the presence of definite psychiatric diagnosis at age 16. However, a statistically significant relationship occurred between temperament and internalized and externalized symptoms. The result analysed by means of step-wise logistic regression have shown that all children with extremely difficult temperament who lived in dysfunctional families, an environment which might be considered as a chronically acting stressor, were diagnosed as having psychiatric disorders. In turn, for children in families with superior behaviour control functioning there was no difference in psychiatric outcome between easy and difficult temperament. This study exemplifies the powerful role of interaction between temperament and environment in determining consequences of experienced stress. Carey (1989), introduced the concept of temperament risk factor (TRF). Strelau (1989), modified the concept of TRF. According to him temperament risk factor is any temperamental trait or configuration of traits that in interaction with other factors acting excessively, persistently or recurrently increase the risk of developing behaviour disorders or pathology or which favours the molding of a maladjusted personality.

Maziade (1988), Pellegrini (1990), and Rutter (1991), in their studies on contribution of temperament to unfavourable consequences of the state of stress accept temperament as one of the many risk factors that contribute to behaviour disorders. Rutter (1991), studied protective factors in children's responses to stress, has shown the powerful influence of increasing number of risk factors for the epidemiology of behaviour disorders. Kyrios and Prior (1990), postulated a theoretical model for the development of early childhood behavoural disturbances in which among other risk factors such as childhood stress, child health problems, parental adjustment, developmental influences, child rearing practices and language abilities, the place of temperament in codetermining behavioural disorders has been shown.

A longitudinal study conducted by Kyrios and Prior (1990), on 3-4 year old children and based on a stress relieving model of temperament, has shown the moderating role of high reactivity low-manageability and low self-regulation in behavioural adjustment under family stressors. Using a broad statistical approach, which was comprised of factor analysis, correlational procedures, multiple regression and path analysis of the obtained data the authors arrived at the conclusion that temperament characteristics are the most predictive variables of child behavioural adjustment. Low self regulation and high reactivity, low manageability regarded in Kyrios Prior study as TRFS, contributing most to the variance of behavioural disturbances at the age of 3-4 years and high reactivity, low manageability was the strongest predictor of behavioural maladjustment at the age of 4-5 years. In his study, Windle (1989), has shown that among five temperament factors: extraversion, emotional stability, activity, adaptability and task orientation, in late adolescents and early adults, it was mainly emotional instability and introversion that were the strongest predictors of mental health as composed of such factors as anxiety, depression, loss of control and emotional ties.

Early research indicated that aspects of personality/temperament such as perceived control might play a significant role, but the findings have been equivocal. Kobasa's (1979), research on hardiness suggested that having an internal locus of control may serve as a buffer against stress, but when situational control is taken into account, having an internal locus of control has been shown to be associated with greater susceptibility to stress amongst subjects who experienced high levels of uncontrollable life events (Meadows, 1989).

Totman et. al. (1980), Broadbent et. al. (1984), in their research illustrated that greater susceptibility to experimental infection have been reported amongst highly aroused introverts as compared to extroverts. More carefully controlled studies of Cohen, Tyrrell and Smith (1993), have questioned these findings.

Roger and Raine (1984), examined measures of stimulus intensity control in the context of stress. Stimulus intensity control includes indices such as neuroticism, extraversion, sensation seeking and augmenting reducing, which are thought to reflect underlying differences in basal cognitive or emotional arousal and arousability.

Roger (1988, 1992), while studying role of personality/temperament in stress and illness, proposed an alternative model based on emotion control and emotional rumination or rehearsal. A number of researchers like Cameron and Meichenbaum (1982), suggested that continued rumination over emotional distress might contribute to delayed recovery. The probability of behaviour disorders increases with the number of risk factors taken into account. When number of risk factors acting jointly extended to four or more the rate of behaviour disorders increased to 20 percent. This finding is a strong argument for taking into account, temperament as one of the many possible risk factors contributing to psychological, psychophysiological and pathological consequences of stress.

A decrease in performance, resulting from a deviation from the optimal level of arousal is an indicator of a state of stress. Dozens of studies have shown that temperament characteristics especially, extraversion and neuroticism (Eysenck, 1970; Eysenck and Eysenck, 1985; Goh and Farley, 1977), strength of nervous system or reactivity (Strelau, 1983, 1988, 2001; Zawadzki, 1991), play an important role as performance moderators. It is highly probable that temperament dimensions, which differ not only in terms of arousal components and emotion oriented tendencies, but represent a whole spectrum of qualitatively different behaviour characteristics play a different role in regulating the demand capability balance depending on the kind of stress taken into account. It might be assumed that moderatory role of temperament may be specific, depending on whether one takes into account stress at work, community stress, natural or technical disasters, acculturative stress or stress resulting from everyday life events.

Strelau, 1985, 1987; Strelau and Eysenck, 1987, explored several dimensions of personality/temperament that refer to the concept of arousal and arousability. They concentrate on different anatomical and physiological mechanisms underlying arousal as well as on different aspects of behaviour in which arousal is expressed. Such dimensions include extraversion introversion, sensation seeking, anxiety, neuroticism, augmenting reducing, strength of nervous system and reactivity.

Eysenck (1967, 1970), illustrated reticulo-cortical arousal loop as the physiological mechanism of extroversion introversion. Extraverts are characterized as having generally lower level of arousability as compared with introverts. From the research findings of Lazarus, 1966; Lundberg, 1982; and Selye, 1975, it is evident that there is a close relationship between the individual's level of arousal, the stimulative value of the threatening situation and the state of stress.

Regulative theory of temperament Strelau (1983 a, 1983 b), pays special attention to traits that refer to energetic aspects of behaviour, reactivity and activity. Many experiments were conducted in Strelau's laboratory by Danilova (1985), Eliasz (1981, 1985), Klonowicz (1974, 1984, 1985), Mundelein (1982), Strelau (1983, 1985), Zumudzki (1986), to see interrelations between reactivity trait and resistance to stress and the ways of coping with stress. It is expected, under demands of highly stimulative value the level of performance in high and low reactive individuals will be different in favour of low reactives. The data generally show that low reactives apparently benefit from the fact that additional stimulation was imposed over a monotonous task, high reactives were adversely affected by both the intensity of stimulation and its nature. Variable stimulation (street noise) produced more deficits in performance than invariant (white noise) stimulation.

Many temperament researchers like Buss and Plomin (1984), Eysenck (1970), Strelau (1994), and Zuckerman (1994), concluded that genetic endowment plays an essential role in determining the variance of temperamental traits. On similar lines, Kendler and Eaves (1986), when exemplifying the contribution of genes to liability of psychiatric disorders, referred to such temperament traits as impulsivity and emotional instability as being influenced by genes, thus contributing, in interaction with predisposing environment, to illness.

Kohn, Lafreniere and Gurevich (1991), showed that trait anxiety and hassles contributed to perceived stress, accounting for over 50 percent of the variance in stress reactions. This study was conducted on 200 undergraduate students and anxiety was measured by means of Spielberger's State Trait Anxiety Inventory. They demonstrated the moderating effect of temperament on stress and the consequences of stress in undergraduate students. Hassles and trait anxiety both contributed to perceived stress, hassles and temperament reactivity both had significant impact on minor ailment, and hassles and trait anxiety had a significant effect on psychiatric symptomatology.

In Horvath and Zuckerman's (1994), study on 500 undergraduate students, sensation seeking as measured by means of SSS-Form V was shown to be a good predictor of risky behaviours as assessed by the general risk appraisal scale.

Watson and Clark (1984), reported that neuroticism should be regarded as a tendency to experience distress even in the absence of stressors, due to the disposition to experience negative emotional states. Similar findings were reported by Bolger (1990) who conducted a study on 166 married couples, who judged for six weeks the experience of daily distress to daily stressors by means of a diary method. The results show that neuroticism is strongly related to experienced distress to daily stressors.

2. Coping styles and Temperament: Coping with stress is understood as a regulatory function that consists of maintaining the adequate balance (or of reducing the discrepancy) between demands and capacities. Review of literature gives support for the two following relationships between temperament and coping: (1) temperament codetermines the amount of effort allocated in performing given activity and (2) temperament by regulating the stimulative value of the conditions or activity under which coping occurs, moderates the conservation of resources.

In several temperament theories the assumption that temperament plays an important role in moderating stress is incorporated as one of the most important postulates. Kagan (1983), considered two types of temperament: inhibited and uninhibited as representing different vulnerability to experience stress under situations of unexpected or unpredictable events. According to Nebylitsyn (1972b), and Strelau (1983), the functional significance of temperament is evident when individuals are confronted with extreme situations or demands.

Why temperamental traits should be considered as important variables moderating stress phenomena? Being more or less unspecific rather formal characteristics, they penetrate all kinds of behaviour, whatever the content or direction of this behaviour. In so doing they contribute to a variety of stress phenomena that may be characterized by means of energy and time. Many temperamental characteristics are related to emotions, as expressed in a tendency to generate emotional processes (Strelau, 1987). As commonly accepted (Lazarus, 1991, 1993) emotions are one of the core constructs for understanding stress.

There exist link between temperament and such stress-related phenomena as the state of stress, coping with stress and psychophysiological and psychological costs of the state of stress. Strelau (1995), considers that stress is a state that is characterized by strong negative emotions, such as fear, anxiety, anger, hostility or other emotional states evoking distress, accompanied by physiological and biochemical changes that evidently exceed the baseline level of arousal. Lazarus (1993), does not recognize the place of arousal as a component of stress, and reduces state of stress to emotions.

Researchers on stress differ mostly with regard to the causes determining the state of stress. Strelau (1988, 1995, 2001), considers 'the state of stress is caused by the lack of equilibrium (occurrence of discrepancy) between demands and individual's capability (capacity) to cope with them'. Such a conceptualization of stress can also be found in the work of Krohne and Laux, 1982; McGrath, 1970; Schulz and Schonpflug, 1982. The magnitude of the state of stress is a function of the size of discrepancy between the demands and capacities, assuming the individual motivated to cope with the demands with which he or she is confronted. The state of stress is a result of interaction between real or perceived demands and individual's response capability as it exists in reality or as they perceive it.

In spite of large number of studies conducted with respect to coping, not much attention has been paid to the role of temperament or personality as a moderator of coping. In distinction to the term 'mediator' the construct 'moderator' refers to and antecedent condition that interacts with other conditions in producing given phenomena in this case the process of coping with stress (Folkman and Lazarus, 1988). Researches relating the role of temperament in coping with stress have followed two different approaches: a) Coping as a process that shapes emotions and b) Coping in terms of resource management processes.

More recently, stress research at York University, has included measures of coping style. Coping inventories have typically isolated three coping 'domains' involving rational, emotional and avoidance strategies (Endler and Parker, 1990). However, using a 'scenario' techniques Roger, Jarvis and Najarian (1993), generated a new item pool which resulted in extraction of an additional domain labeled detachment. The scenarios comprised description of emotional situations to which the subjects were asked to respond by listing ways in which they would cope with these predicaments. A validation study of the four-factor coping style questionnaire (CSQ) Roger et. al. (1993), showed that rational and detached coping correlated to form an adaptive coping style domain. Emotional and avoidance coping correlated positively to form a maladaptive coping style domain and these adaptive and maladaptive clusters were inturn inversely correlated with one another.

Lazarus (1993), assumes that the temperament traits cannot be neutral for the ongoing effort to manage specific demands appraised as taxing or overwhelming. Folkman and Lazarus (1985), are of the view that the differences among the two basic coping style: action and emotion oriented depend on personality and temperamental dimensions. But also, if we consider coping in terms of style, the individual applies in order to change the unfavourable person-environment relationship (Folkman and Lazarus, 1985, 1988), then it can be hypothesized that whether problem focused coping or emotion focused coping develops depends to some extent on the moderating role of temperament characteristics.

Strelau and Szczepaniak (1994), in a study to relate selected temperament characteristics to coping styles used revised EPQ-R – Eysenck and Barrett (1985), and the preliminary version of Formal Characteristics of Behaviour-Temperament Inventory (FCB-TI; Strelau and Zawadzki, 1993). Coping style was measured by Coping Inventory for Stressful Situations (CISS; Endler and Parker, 1990), which allows the assessment of three coping styles: task oriented, emotion oriented and avoidance oriented. The results of this study show, task oriented coping style correlated positively with extraversion and briskness (action oriented temperament characteristics). In turn emotion oriented coping style was positively related to emotion centered temperament characteristics, such as neuroticism, perseverance and emotional reactivity. Also the social diversion component of the avoidance oriented coping style showed relationship with temperamental traits (extraversion, activity) consistent with hypotheses. These results with respect to relationship between Eysenckian temperament characteristics and coping styles replicate the findings reported in the literature (see Bolger, 1990; Endler and Parker, 1990; Parkes 1986).

In a study Strelau and Zawadzki (1995), factor analysed, data on temperament and coping style and extracted three factors: Factor I identified as emotion oriented coping has high loadings on temperament traits that refer to emotions (perseverance, emotional reactivity) and high loadings with opposite sign on traits mobility and endurance. Factor II referring to action-oriented coping has the highest loading on the briskness, which are composed of tempo and speed. Factor III which represents avoidance-oriented coping has a high loading on the activity scale. This coping style is composed of distraction and social diversion, coping by social diversion needs to be active.

Hobfoll (1989), viewed coping as resource management process that proposes to move from coping as a regulator that shapes emotions to coping that consists of replacement, substitution and investment of resources. The degree to which an individual is engaged in coping with stress can be characterized by means of extent intensity and persistence with which resources are allocated and consumed. This approach allows us to look at temperament as a moderator of coping, from a different perspective.

Schonpflug (1987), has shown how temperamental traits may contribute to effort expenditure. This core concept in Schonpflug's approach has been considered by him as a quantitative dimension of coping involvement. Effort expenditure comprises all three formal characteristics of allocation and consumption of resources-intensity, extent and persistence. Schonpflug has shown the place of temperament in effort regulation in two contexts:

1. Temperament traits are codeterminants of the amount of effort allocated in task performance. Effort is expressed in terms of subjective ratings, behavioural involvement and level of arousal or biochemical changes.

2. Temperament as a regulator of the stimulative value of the conditions or activity under which coping occurs, moderates the conservation of resources. Schonpflug refers to the concept of 'style of action' developed by Strelau (1983), on the basis of Tomaszewski (1978), distinction between basic and auxiliary actions. Style of action is the typical manner in which an action is performed by the individual, develops under environmental influences on the basis of temperament endowment especially, reactivity. According to Tomaszewski (1978), auxiliary actions lower the risk of failure in task performance under stress. Using Hobfoll's (1989), and Schonpflug's (1987), terminology, one may say that auxiliary action contributes to the conservation of resources. Activities that lead directly to the attainment of a certain goal should be regarded as basic. 'Considering the relation between auxiliary and basic actions from the point of view of intensity of stimulation means that auxiliary actions, by safeguarding, facilitating or simplifying the basic ones, lower the stimulative value of activity or of the situation in which the activity is performed' (Strelau, 1988). High reactive individuals show adjunctive style and low reactive individuals show straightforward style of action.

Thus coping styles/strategies viewed in terms of style of action, and strongly related to temperament may be considered as moderators of conservation of resources aimed at avoiding or reducing the state of stress. Highly reactive individuals by means of the auxiliary style, perform more action as compared with low reactive subjects, thus they allocate more resources in order to cope with stress. On the other hand, by allocating more resources in auxiliary actions, they avoid failures and maintain an adequate level of efficiency in task performance under highly stimulative situations. This in turn may be considered to be a gain of resources.

In many studies independent of the population (children, adolescents or adults) and type of task under investigation (mental work or motor performance), the results show under demands of high stimulative value for high reactive individuals the dominance of the adjunctive style assures efficient functioning. For low reactive individuals in contrast the prevalence of the straightforward style results in better functioning under stress (Strelau, 1983, 1988, 2001). These finding have also been supported in Schonpflug's laboratory by Mundelein, 1982; Schonpflug and Mundelein, 1986; and Schulz, 1986.

The understanding of stress as an outcome of the interaction between the individual and the stress-inducing environment implicates the importance of individual differences in research on stress. The process of appraisal of perceived situation, treated as the most important factor in determining stress, is always a subjective one, thus being different in different people. There exist also individual differences in reactions to stress as well as in coping with stress.

A special place in codetermining the state of stress is given to personality and temperament dimensions in which individuals differ. Temperament dimension, reactivity is regarded important source of variance in most of the aspects of stress. Parkes (1986), in a study applied an interactional paradigm to study how 135 first year female student nurses coped with stressful episodes. Such variables as environmental factors, situational characteristics, temperament traits and coping styles were taken into account. Parkes found that extraversion and neuroticism together with enviornmental and situational factors predicted coping styles. Direct coping was typical for extraversion, whereas, suppression occurred together with neuroticism.

Vingerhoets et. al. (1993), in a study, in which apart from personality variables, the Pavlovian temperament traits were under control, showed that weeping in women, considered as emotion focused coping was negatively related to strength of excitation and strength of inhibition. Women occupying a high position on weeping dimension were characterized by both weak excitation and weak inhibition of the nervous system.

3. Stress and coping styles: In general, it is believed that the state of stress is caused by lack of equilibrium, occurrence of discrepancy between demands and individual's capability or capacity to cope with them (Strelau, 1988). Such a conceptualization of stress is also found in literature, e.g., McGrath (1970); Krohne and Laux (1982); Schulz and Schonpflug (1982); Ratajczak and Adamiec (1989). The magnitude of the state of stress is a function of the size of discrepancy between the demands and capacities, assuming the individual is motivated to cope with the demands with which he or she is confronted.

Holmes and Rahe (1967), in their study, show that there is a high degree of consensus among the experts about significance of life events. Demands that exist objectively act independently of the individual's perception. This refers to extreme life changes such as death, bereavement, disaster and war. The correlation of about 0.90 exist across age, sex, marital status and education, in the intensity and time necessary to accommodate to specify life events speaks in favour of universal stressors. Studies conducted by Aldwin, Levenson, Spiro and Bosse, 1989; Pellegrini, 1990; Freedy, Kilpatrick and Resnick, 1993; provide empirical evidence and support to Holmes and Rahe.

In general it is viewed that individual's capability to cope with demands depends on the following characteristics: intelligence, special abilities, skills, knowledge, personality and temperamental traits, features of the physical makeup, experience with stress inducing situations, coping strategies and actual physical and psychic state of the individual.

Selye (1956, 1982), considers nonspecificity of demands (stressors) and the nonspecific response to these demands (stress) as the essence of his theory. As selye writes: 'It is immaterial whether the agent or situation we face is pleasant or unpleasant; all that counts is the intensity of the demand for readjustment or adaptation', (Selye, 1975). Thus intensity of demand is a crucial factor causing stress. Deprivation of stimuli and excessive stimulation are both accompanied by an increase in stress, sometimes to the point of distress.

Lundberg (1982), McGrath (1970), and Weick (1970), also consider intensity of stimulation as a source of stress. Situation or stimuli above and below the individual's need for stimulation, evoke a state of discomfort, the state of stress, which leads to changes in physiological, psychological and behavioural reactions as well as in the level of performance.

Understanding stress in terms of resources which has become more recently a popular view (e.g., Hobfoll 1988, 1989, 1991; Schonpflug, 1987, 1993; Schonpflug and Battman, 1987) potential or actual loss of valued resources regarded here as the cause of the state of stress, can be understood only if we take into account the interaction between invested and gained resources. Resources are defined as those objects, personal characteristics, conditions or energies (Hobfoll, 1989). Loss or lack of gain is regarded as a source of stress. Regarding stress from another perspective, in regulating the balance between resources allocated and resources gained. In the case of objective stressors, threat and harm (threat of loss of resources) are incorporated into population specific interaction between the individual and life events.

The state of stress is inseparable from coping. Vitaliano et. al. (1990), treat coping with stress as a regulatory function that consists of maintaining the adequate balance between demands and capacities or of reducing the discrepancy between demands and capacities. Efficient coping, which results in match or goodness of fit between demands and capacities, reduces the state of stress, whereas, inefficient coping leads to the increase of the state of stress. Schonpflug and Battman (1987), understand coping in terms of resolving the state of stress from point of view of resource management process in terms of gains and loss.

Cohn and Lazarus (1979), Moss and Schaefer (1986), Pearlin and Schooler (1978), suggest some commonly used methods of coping. These are direct action, seeking information, turning to others, resigned acceptance, emotional discharge and intrapsychic processes. In order to study consistency in the way people cope with particular type of stressor Stone and Neale (1984), conducted a study. They observed that people use just one method of coping, rather than a combination of strategies.

Reviews of researches on stress coping suggest to conclude that people use different coping strategies to reduce the potential for stress. These are enhancing social support, improving one's personal control and hardiness, focusing, reconstructing stressful situations, compensating through self improvement, organizing one's world better, exercising to increase fitness, preparing for stressful events.

Broadhead et. al. (1983), Wortman et. al. (1987), in their study on enhancing social support as a dynamic process found that people's need for giving of and receipt of the support change over time. Some factors within the individual determine whether he or she will receive or provide social support when it is needed. One factor is temperament. People differ in their need for and interest in social contact and affiliation.

Fischman (1987), and Kobasa (1986), reviewed the literature on improving one's personal control and hardiness. They are of the view that the process of personal control begins very early. Parents and teachers show a child their love and respect and provide a stimulating environment, encourage and praise the child's accomplishments and set reasonable standards of conduct and performance that he or she can regard as challenge rather than threat. Personal control is an important component of hardiness and people can be trained to become hardier. Salvatore Maddi and Suzanne Kobasa have designed a program that consists of three techniques. Focusing on various body sensations can help identify at times of stress and the source of stress. In reconstructing stressful situations the individual thinks about a recent stressful situation and makes two lists: ways it could have turned out better, ways it might have turned out worse. It allows a person to examine alternative courses of action and realize that it could be worse. While compensating through self improvement people generally come out of challenging situation successfully, it reassures them that they can still cope.

Lakein, 1973, (in Sarafino 1990 p155), while conducting a study on organizing one's world better proposed that a place for everything and everything in its place or putting materials in alphabetized file folders or organizing one's world reduces frustration, wastage of time and potential for stress. Time management i.e., organizing one's time consists of three elements. First, to set goals that are reasonable and obtainable as well as short term and long term goals. Second, making daily 'to do lists' with priorities indicated, keeping the goals in mind. Third, to set up a schedule for the day, allocating estimated time periods to each item in the list.

Kobasa, Maddi and Puccetti (1982), conducted a study on exercising to increase fitness. They are of the view that exercise and physical fitness can protect people from harmful effects of stress. It also develops intellectual functioning and personal control to decrease anxiety, depression, hostility and tension. It prevents people from developing stress-related illness. Kobasa et. al. (1982), reported that men who scored higher on a survey of their exercise reported less illness.

Janis (1958), pioneered the psychological study of the need to prepare people for stressful events such as surgery. Janis proposed that some degree of anticipatory worry about stressful event is adaptive because it motivates coping. It is a three step procedure; first, receiving information about the event; second, developing expectations by rehearsing the event mentally; third, by mobilizing coping techniques in an effort to become reassured of a successful outcome. These findings are supported by many researchers like Anderson and Masur (1983); Johnson (1983). All these methods are useful and helpful in reducing the potential for stress.

While describing models of coping, Lazarus (1981), identified four basic ways of coping: direct actions, intrapsychic strategies, inhibition and information seeking. In their study Folkman and Lazarus (1985), discussed eight different aspects of coping on the basis of which they developed corresponding measuring scales. These are confrontive coping, distancing, self-control, seeking social support, accepting responsibility, escape-avoidance, planful problem solving and positive appraisal.

Lyne and Roger (2000), while reassessing psychometric properties of COPE questionnaire concluded that coping process involves a three-factor structure i.e., rational coping, emotion focussed coping and avoidance coping.

Carver et. al. (1989), have described fourteen discreet styles of coping: active coping, planning, suppressing completing activities, restraint coping, seeking social support for instrumental reasons, seeking social support for emotional reasons, positive reinterpretation and growth, acceptance, turning to religion, focusing on the venting emotion, denial, behavioural disengagement, mental disengagement and a single item measure of alcohol drug disengagement.

Endler and Parker (1990), proposed a three-factor structure for their multidimension coping inventory (MCI), which they labeled: Task, Emotional and Avoidance coping. Roger, Jarvis and Najarian (1993), extracted rational, emotional and avoidance coping for their coping style questionnaire (CSQ) but with an addition detachment scale.

In a structural analysis of COPE questionnaire Ingledew et. al. (1996), located three second order factors which were labeled as problem focused coping, avoidance coping and lack of emotion focused coping. This result was similar to second order analysis reported by Carver et. al. (1989), but based on slight differences in subscales, with a new scale for humour and no scale for religion.

The three factor results for COPE serve to confirm an emerging pattern in the literature. In the Ways of Coping Questionnaire (Folkman and Lazarus, 1988), coping is seen as comprising problem focused and emotion focused strategies. The Multidimensional Coping Inventory (MCI; Endler and Parker, 1990) consists of three factors: Task, Emotion and Avoidance coping, a pattern, which was closely replicated by Olff, Brosschot and Godaert (1993). Similarly, second order factor analysis of COPE by Carver et. al. (1989), gave four factors labeled: task, emotion, avoidance and cognitive coping. In the development of coping style questionnaire (CSQ), Roger et. al. (1993), described four strategies labeled as rational, emotional, avoidance and detached coping.

4. Stress and Emotional Control : In a study conducted by Manhas (2003) on coping strategies among Kashmiri migrant children, she found that coping mechanisms shown by children were quite similar to the ones adopted by their parents. Different coping strategies in children were facilitated or made more difficult by the support or disapproval of the parents respectively. There children exhibit a multiplicity of coping mechanisms. Sane child uses different coping strategies simultaneously. These finding are in tune with findings of Jacobsen and Krogh (1992) and also those of Almqvist and Hwang (1999). Coping strategies used by the children were not centered towards solving the problems but rather had a strong emotional quality altitude to it since they can not change their situation they tend to give high emotional tone to their adaptive behaviour. These results are also similar to those of Brotman and Wiesz (1988) and Almqvist and Hwang (1999), who assert that such children who have less opportunity to improve their living conditions rely on emotion focused coping to a greater degree.

Roger 1988; Roger and Jamieson 1988, suggested that individuals differences in emotional control patterns serve to either prolong or attenuate physiological recovery from stress, particularly the degree to which individuals mentally rehearse past failures and engage himself/herself denigrating thoughts. Individuals who are more likely to mentally rehearse failures may be those who have low self esteem and are less positive about themselves, thus show low expectation for success.

Rector, Roger and Nussbaum (1993), in a research on 182 students studied moderating role of self esteem in emotional control strategies and health. They found that subjects with low self esteem rehearse and inhibit expression of emotion. Where as high self esteem correlation positively with detached and ratio al coping styles i.e. adaptive coping strategies.

Roger and Schapals (1996) conducted a study on 263 undergraduate students to find how repression sensitization and emotional control are related. Significant correlations have been found between rehearsal and social sensitivity. Benign control has been found to correlate inversely and significantly with extraversion and confidence, which is an index of sociality.

McDougall et. al. (1991) conducted a study on 41 male young offenders to see relationship between aggression, anger control and emotional control. Rehearsal was found to correlate with neuroticism, anxiety and somatic tension. Rehearsing or ruminating about upsetting events may generate somatic tension which may be reduced by engaging in emotionally expressive behaviour including aggression.

Roger and Najarian (1998) conducted a study on 74 nursing students to see relationship between emotional rumination & cortisol secretion under stress. The results show that rehearsal was significantly related to cortisol change index derived from urine sample. ECQ is emotional inhibition and EPI is neuroticism & social sensitivity components were found to relate significantly to cortisol secretion to a lesser extent.

Roger et. al. (2001) explored cross-cultural differences in emotional control, using emotional control questionnaire. The ECQ has been extensively validated on English and Spanish. The rumination and emotional inhibition factors also replicated well in Korean sample. But for Benign control this was not the case. The differences for Korean sample as compared with English and Spanish sample indicate cultural differences. Koreans consider anger as negative and in appropriate behaviour. Thus emotional inhibition & rumination are validated factors.

5. Stress and Type-A behaviour pattern: The sequal of studies relating Type-A Behaviour Pattern (TABP) present an evidence that individuals who exhibit the Type-A behaviour pattern react differently to stressors than those with Type-B behaviour pattern. Carver et. al. (1985), and Glass (1977), propose that Type-A individuals respond more quickly and strongly to stress, often interpreting stressors as threats to their personal control. Byrne and Rosenman (1986), and Smith and Anderson (1986), are of the view that Type-A behaviour pattern may have another kind of impact on stress: the Type-A pattern may actually increase the person's likelihood of encountering stressful events.

It has also been noted that Type-A individuals tend to seek out demanding situations in their lives (Suls and Sanders, 1988). What is more, people who are often in a hurry and impatient with delays – as is the case for Type-A individuals, tend to have more accidents than people who are more easy going. In these ways the Type-A and B patterns can affect the transactions of people in their environment and modify the stress they experience in their lives.

Matthews (1986), proposed that people's response to stress or strain includes both psychological and physiological components. The physiological portion of the response to stress is called reactivity, which is measured against a basline or resting level of arousal. Do Type-A individuals show greater reactivity than Type-Bs? In general, yes. Glass et. al. (1980), examined the reactivity of men who each completed in a video game against an individual who was a confederate of the researchers. Although the instructions indicated that the winner would receive a prize, the game was rigged so that subject could never win. The subjects were assigned to two groups, Type-A and Type-B, on the basis of their performance in the structured interview. Half of the men in each group played the game while being harassed and insulted by the confederates, for the remaining subjects, the confederate was silent. Several physiological measures were used, including blood pressure, heart rate and plasma catecholamine levels. In the absence of harassment, both Type-A and Type-B subjects showed substantial and equal increases in physiological arousal over their baseline levels. But in the harassment condition, the Type-A subjects showed greater reactivity than the Type-Bs did.

Many other studies, Carver, Diamond and Humphries (1985), Contrada and Krantz (1988) and Houston (1986), have also compared the reactivity of Type-A and Type-B people, using male and female subjects and a variety of tasks, ways to induce stress and measures of Type-A and Type-B behaviour. Most of these studies have found greater reactivity among Type-A individuals especially, males.

A number of other researchers Lawler et. al. (1981), Lundberg (1986), Matthews and Jennings (1984), and Thoresen and Pattillo (1988), have examined reactivity in Type-A and Type-B boys and girls and found result similar to those found with adults. This suggests that the tendency of Type-A individuals to be highly reactive to stress may begin in childhood.

Some researches e.g. Contrada et. al. (1988), Krantz and Durel (1983), Krantz et. al. (1987), suggest the intriguing possibility that people's Type-A behaviour may, in part, be caused by their physiological responses to stress. Two lines of evidence seem to support this view. First, research has been conducted with Type-A patients who were either taking or not taking beta-blockers a class of drugs that dampens sympathetic nervous system transmission. This research by Krantz et. al. (1982), demonstrated that Type-A patients who were taking a beta-blocker exhibited less Type-A behaviour in structured interview than those who were not taking the drug. In a second study, Kahn et. al. (1980), have examined the blood pressure of Type-A and Type-B patients under general anesthesia at the start of coronary bypass surgery. Compared with Type-Bs, Type-A patients showed greater blood pressure increases over the pressure measured when they were admitted to the hospital. This is important because research showing greater reactivity in Type-A than Type-B individuals was typically done with subjects who could use conscious appraisal processes to judge the situation as stressful. Since all the bypass patients were unconscious during the operation, the results with these patients indicate that the Type-A person's greater reactivity to stress can occur without the role of conscious processes. Taken together these lines of evidence suggest that physiological reactions to stressors can influence Type-A behaviour.

Margolis et. al. (1983), studied relationships between psycho-social factors and Type-A behaviour. They stated this relationship to be very complex and seem to involve multiple levels of human experience. We can use a system or ecological approach with four levels: (a) intrapersonal level (b) interpersonal level (c) institutional level (d) cultural level.

The first level is intrapersonal: within the person, there are many psychological factors that relate to Type-A behaviour. One of these factors is personal control. David Glass (1977), has proposed that Type-A behaviour may represent an effort by individuals to control stressful experiences in their lives. Research has generally supported this view (Matthews, 1982).

At the interpersonal level social processes and Type-A behaviour affect each other. In a study, the impact of the Type-A behaviour pattern on social interaction was demonstrated by Van Egeren, Sniderman and Roggelin (1982), in which paired subjects could either cooperate or compete in a game. The pairs of subjects consisted of either two Type-A college students or two Type-Bs. The Type-A pair showed more competition and less cooperation than the Type-B pairs. In their study Carver and Glass (1978), found that being insulted increases the hostility and aggression of both Type-A and Type-B subjects, but the effect is much greater for Type-A individuals.

Smith and Anderson (1986), are of the view that in general, people who display Type-A behaviour tend to elicit reactions from others that create more demands and stimulate more Type-A behaviour. The third level is institutional and includes the experiences of people in educational and occupational settings. There are several ways these experiences can foster Type-A, behaviour. One way involves reward structures that promote aggressive competition, as can happen when many individuals are vying for a small number of rewards such as job promotion or high grades. Another way involves time or work demand by a boss or teacher that encourage the feeling of time urgency. Lovallo et. al. (1986), in their research have shown that Type-A individuals exhibit greater reactivity to stress than Type-Bs during final exam in medical school. Sorensen et. al. (1987), in their research study found that employees with high scores on the Jenkins Activity survey for Type-A behaviour have longer work hours and less supportive relationships with co-workers than Type-B workers do.

The fourth level of relationship between psychosocial factors and Type-A behaviour is cultural. Some cultures place greater emphasis than others on the work ethics, getting ahead, status and accumulating goods that reflect status. Margolis et. al. (1983), in their reserch found that people in cultures that emphasize these values are likely to display more Type-A behaviour than those who live in cultures that do not.

Eliasz (1981), and Strelau (1983), while conducting research on temperament consider temperament risk factors (TRF) to be any temperamental trait or configuration of traits that in interaction with other factors acting persistently or recurrently (social environment, educational treatment, situations or individual's characteristics like Type-A behaviour pattern etc.) increases the probability of developing disorders or anomalies in behaviour or that favours the moulding of a maladjusted personality.

Strelau and Eliasz (1994), consider that stress and anxiety in high reactive individuals with high scores on TABP should be regarded as the psycho-physiological costs these individuals pay for performing activity whose stimulating value is beyond their temperamental capacity.

Identifying components of Type-A behaviour as toxic and nontoxic achieving, Birks and Roger (2000), concluded that achievement motivation is divisible into these two components. This distinction should allow a much better understanding of how individual differences might confer protection or risk during exposure to stress. Factor analysis of Jenkins Activity survey by Pred, Spence and Helmreich (1986), yielded two factors labeled Impatience Irritability (II) and Achievement Striving (AS). Subsequent work by Barling et. al. (1990), Helmreich et. al. (1988), and Pred et. al. (1986), suggested that achievement striving factor was associated with positive performance and satisfaction indices and could be regarded as nontoxic whereas, the toxic Impatience Irritability component was associated with physical and mental health complaint and dissatisfaction. However, the AS and II components assess only two of the behaviours thought to characterize Type-A, and Matthews, Glass, Rosenman and Bortner (1977), have argued that anger, potential for hostility and competitiveness are the key characteristics in predicting coronary heart disease (CHD).

Toxic achieving correlated significantly and positively with rehearsal in both scales 'student version' and 'working people version'. Rehearsal has been shown to be related to worse health status in an undergraduate population (Roger et. al. 1994), physiological indices of adaptation (Roger and Jamieson, 1988) and potentially compromised immune function as observed in urinary cortisol (Roger, 1988). Since this is such a well-validated measure of maladaptive behaviour it is encouraging to find its relationship with 'Toxic Achieving' to be significant. Since rehearsal can be defined as the preoccupation with emotionally upsetting events, these finding are intuitively consistent: if one is unable to forget about an incident which has been upsetting this would be maladaptive and if the situation were concerned with failure to achieve a goal, then such an attitude would be toxic within the toxic achieving framework.

Llyod and Cawley (1983), point to the existence of a coronary prone personality that can be identified long before an attack occurs. The most important trait in the coronary prone person is the existence of the Type-A pattern, especially, impatience and overactivity factors. However, a second cluster seems to be very important. This is the presence of depression and high level of anxiety, which seem to indicate an overactive sympathetic nervous system (Van Doornen, 1980). In addition, it has been suggested that victims of coronary attacks experience no more stressful events than healthy subjects. However, they appear to translate their emotional upsets into bodily symptoms more frequently. As a result they seem to suffer more from digestion and sleep disturbances, which may compound or add to the problems at work. Goldband (1980), and Martin et. al. (1989), have observed this sympathetic reactivity and suggested that Type-A people have an increased risk for a wide variety of stress related illnesses, not just coronary disease.

Lovallo and Pishkin (1980), observed that, Type-A people show greater sympathetic arousal, more clotting of blood, higher cholestrol levels and increased triglyceride levels under stress. Grimm and Yarnold (1984), are of the view that Type-A people do report more stress symptoms than Type-B people. They appear to set higher performance standards for themselves.

Yarnold and Grimm (1982), Van Egeren et. al. (1983), studied interpersonal relations of Type-A and Type-B individuals. In interpersonal relations with Type-B people, Type-A people are much more dominant and are impatient in competitive situations.

Roger (1995), has recently suggested that the disparate findings from studies examining the moderating role of personality/temperament in stress and illness might best be understood by incorporating them into a hierarchical model governed by the higher order construct of self-esteem. In this context toxic Type-A behaviour might be regarded as compensatory reaction to perception of low self worth. Rector et. al. (1993), have already shown that low self-esteem is associated with a greater susceptibility to stress manipulation. Roger (1995), subsequently developed an explanatory model which distinquishes initially between self concept and self esteem, defining the former as a theoretical self construct which is operationalized only when an attitude is held about it. Self-esteem inturn influences other perceptions and behaviours for example distinguishing between toxic Type-A behaviour and nontoxic achievement motivation and between likelihood of rehearsing or not rehearsing.

6. Temperament and Type-A Behaviour Pattern: One of the central issue in temperament research is to show that temperament plays an important role in human adaptation to the environment and in regulating the individual's relationship with the external world, especially, the social surroundings. The functional significance of temperament traits in real human life is best argument for devoting time and effort to studying the nature as well as other aspects of temperament.

Even though Friedman and Rosenman (1958), originally conceived Type-A in terms of a person's interaction with the environment a tendency to behave in hostile, competitive and time urgent ways, when confronted with challenge. Thoreson and Powell (1992), pointed out that most research has taken an overly simplistic approach neglecting the kind of complex reciprocal interactions that are part of everyday life, example, a Type-A person, sensitive to threats of self esteem may react with hostility to implied criticism from others which may then offend others and help create the very kind of social environment the person is uncomfortable in (Smith and Anderson, 1986). This general conceptualization resembles what Wachtel's 'Reciprocal Causuality', both ideas that sensitize up to the constant back and forth nature of human existence.

Dembroski et. al. (1977), are of the view that when challenged, Type-A individuals show more physiological arousal than Type-B individuals. Dembroski and McDougall (1978), further stated that Type-A individuals are more likely to compare themselves with others, and to exhibit exaggerated need for achievement (Burnam et. al., 1975). This heightened need for achievement is an important characteristic of people who exhibit Type-A behaviour.

Lovallo and Pishkin (1980), stated that Type-A people reveal both physical and behavioural traits besides the hurry syndrome that set them apart from their Type-B counterparts. In general Type-A people show greater sympathetic arousal, more clotting of blood, higher cholesterol levels and increased triglyceride levels under stress. They examined the relationship between Type-A characteristics and personality moderators, self-preoccupation. Subjects were administered JAS and Stress symptom rating form. Type-As reported more stress than self-controlled Type-As and Type-Bs.

House et. al. (1982), suggest that central trait of Type-A is his desire for social achievement, reflected in ambition, competitiveness and aggressiveness etc. This trait is analogous to extrinsic motivation for working e.g., desire for money, status and recognition. Friedman and Rosenman (1974), argued that Type-B individuals may be equally or even more ambitious than Type-A, but ambition associated with Type-B is characterized by confidence and satisfaction whereas, ambition associated with Type-A behaviours pattern is dominated by anger and anxiety. Investigations of well being between Type-As and Type-Bs have produced mixed results and suggest that other variables are mediating the relation between Type-A/B and psychological well being. Type-A person possesses personality traits impatience, ambition, competitiveness and aggressiveness that cause self-selection into jobs that entail greater exposure to stressors (Garrity and Marx, 1979).

Hicks et. al. (1982, 1983 a, b), proposed that temperament of Type-A seems to contribute directly to heart disease. In relaxed situations, the hormonal secretions, pulse rate and blood pressure of Type-As and Type-Bs are not different. Krantz and Munuck (1984), stated that when Type-A individuals are harassed, given a difficult challenge or threatened with loss of freedom and control, they are more physiologically reactive. Their hormonal secretion, pulse rate and blood pressure tend to soar whereas, those of Type-Bs remain at moderate levels.

Spielberger (1983), while working on adult population stated that trait anxiety correlates positively and significantly with toxic achieving. High scores on trait anxiety are associated with adjustment problems. Since trait anxiety is a well-validated measure of adaptation, this correlational relationship with toxicity points to the success of toxic achieving as an index of maladaptive attitudes.

Furham et. al. (1985), found that once they have failed to meet these excessive personal standards, Type-As more often engage in self criticism and experience greater feelings of worthlessness and self anger.

A large-scale study conducted by Eliasz and Wrzesniewski (1986, 1988), on 1040 trade and high school students of both sexes aged from 17 to 18 years gives evidence that the shaping of TABP in adolescents is a complex process involving several variables. TABP results from among other things, the interaction between social pressure on an adolescent to maximize achievement (at home and at school) and the individual's temperament. The results show that TABP develops in both high reactive and low reactive individuals; thus there is no direct relation between temperament characteristics (level of reactivity) and TABP. It came out however, that there is an indirect relationship between temperament and TABP. The moulding of TABP develops in HR and LR adolescents under different psycho-physiological costs.

This finding was exemplified from another study representing extreme scores on TABP and trait anxiety. More high reactive adolescents diagnosed as having high scores on TABP are characterized by high level of anxiety than are HR individuals with low scores on TABP. The data conclude that in HR adolescent the development of TABP is mostly accompanied with high level of trait anxiety. One of the constituents of TABP is high need for achievement (n-ach). It motivates the individual towards highly stimulating forms of activity. It follows from the concept of reactivity and activity that this need develops mainly in LR individuals, with high need for stimulation.

In HR individuals the n-achievement is result of external pressure, upbringing at home and education at school. Since the high stimulative value of n-achievement is in dissonance with the low need for stimulation typical of high reactives, submission to social pressure that leads to the development of TABP, takes place at the cost of anxiety. Eliasz and Wrzeniewski (1986), state that anxiety in HR adolescents with high score on TABP should be regarded as the psychophysiological costs these individuals pay for performing activity whose stimulating value is beyond their temperamental capacity.

Smith and Anderson (1986), Strube (1987), on the basis of their studies illustrated that Type-A people are not only reactive, they also seek out challenge, value productivity and success and like to know how well they are doing. Booth-Kewley and Friedman (1987), Matthews (1988), in their research findings reveal that fast paced, time conscious life style and high ambitions are not components of CHD. The crucial component of Type-A that seems to be negative is emotion, especially, the anger associated with an aggressively reactive temperament.

Pred, Spence, Helmreich (1986), noted that frequency of physical complaints was significantly correlated with impatience, irritability but not with achievement strivings. These two relatively independent factors in Type-A, B behaviour pattern have differential effects on performance and health.

Friedman and Kewley (1987), in a review applied a statistical reanalysis to the data of 101 previously published research articles. The goal was to look relationship between temperament/personality (depression, anger/hostility, anxiety, aggression, extroversion) and physical diseases.

Studies reported in literature indicate that TABP may be found also in children and adolescents and that parental and environmental influences are the main antecedents of TABP (e.g., Matthews and Woodal, 1988). Steinberg (1985), has shown that to some extent early temperamental characteristics allow the prediction of TABP in young adulthood. High adaptability and negative mood are associated with achievement striving (AS), one of the crucial component of TABP.

Kuiper and Martin (1989), consider Type-A behaviours are the result of low self-esteem. It is suggested that these dysfunctional attitudes center largely around unrealistic rigid contingencies for evaluating self worth and that primarily these contingencies relate to high standards of performance. If the standards of self-evaluation are perceived as being met the individual maintains a positive self-view, but if not the resulting negative self view may incorporate low self esteem as well as negative affective state. Type-A individuals engage in efforts to establish self-evaluations such as hard driving, competitive and achievement striving behaviours. Type-A are more likely to place blame on environmental factors such as other people, when they fail to reach their goals.

Martin, Kuiper and Westra (1989), gave empirical support for the above view, that increasing Type-A scores were associated with increased dysfunctional attitude endorsement as well as lower levels of self-esteem and higher level of depressive affect.

Edward, Jefferry and Cooper (1990) evaluated seven alternative conceptual models specifying interrelations among stress, personality / temperament, coping and psychological and physical symptoms.

Cofta (1992), and Eliasz and Cofta (1992), confirmed that long lasting dissonance between TABP and high level of reactivity leads to the risk of CHD.

Thoreson and Powell (1992), recently analysed the conceptual as well as empirical issues in Type-A theory and research and concluded that there is much potentially important work to be done with the construct, provided more careful attention is paid to its interaction, cognitive and cultural aspects.

Raikkonen (1992), conducted a longitudinal study on 6 to 9 years old 924 children to study childhood behavioural characteristics and mother – child relation ships as a risk factor for Type-A behaviour in adolescents. The result show that Type-A behaviour in adolescence was an outcome of childhood hyperactivity and hostile maternal – child rearing practices. The results suggest that (a) Type-A pattern in childhood is a certain Type-A prone temperament characterized by hyperactivity and restlessness, (b) instead of attributing the origin of Type-A behaviour to the child, there may be a Type-A precipitating mother.

Roger et. al. (1995), devised their own Type-A index (The York Type-A scale YTAS) comprising three factors: competitive striving (CS), Achievement Motivation (AM) and Anxiety (ANX), where the first and second factors were assumed to be unambiguously toxic and nontoxic respectively. Anxiety factor had high correlation with rehearsal.

Birk and Roger (1998), in their research finding found that rehearsal was significantly related in predicted direction (negatively), to nontoxic achieving. This negative relationship makes intuitive sense since rehearsal is a measure of maladaptive behaviour and nontoxic achieving of adaptation, thus they would be negatively related. The small but significant correlation between detachment and nontoxic achieving was of greater magnitude. Degree of detachment would be necessary in individuals who are capable of nontoxic achievement.

Roger, Nash and Najarian (1995), conducted study to see correlation between self esteem and Type-A behaviour pattern, initial correlational analyses show that general self esteem factor correlated significantly and inversely with York Type-A competitive striving factor and with anxiety factor but only marginally with the achievement motivation factor.

Roger (1996), conducted a study to see role of cognitive rumination, emotional inhibition and rehearsal in affecting health status. His findings are in consonance with Kaiser et. al. (1995). The findings show that personality variables most likely to influence health are primarily concerned with emotional style and coping. Tendency to inhibit emotion, to engage in emotional rumination, emotional over involvement are related significantly to deterioration in health.

The extent to which the personality measures might be in corporated into a single index of risk was explored by conducting factor analysis of major dimensions, which contribute to variance in health status and social adjustment. A factor comprising the personal locus of control, rational coping and benign control remained intact across extractions. Thus first factor combined self-esteem, interpersonal locus of control, detached coping, rehearsal, emotional inhibition, avoidance coping and toxic TABP.

Birks and Rogers (2000), while identifying components of Type-A behaviour: toxic and nontoxic achieving propose that Type-A research has tended to focus on working populations, but it is unlikely that Type-A behaviour originates in work experience and should therefore be apparent in non working students population.

However, while the basic elements of the construct would be common to both groups, the situations, which would elicit Type-A responses, are likely to be different and separate questionnaires are used for different populations. Students toxic achieving questionnaire and Working adult achieving questionnaire yielded two factor structure, which could unambiguously be labeled Toxic Achieving (TA) and Nontoxic Achieving (NTA), distinction between them, was confirmed by validation data. These showed that TA and NTA were inversely correlated and correlated in opposite direction with two independent measures of toxic Type-A behaviour MTABS (Burns and Bluen 1992), and a scale devised by Roger et. al. (1995).

CHAPTER – III
METHODOLOGY

METHODOLOGY

The present chapter deals with the methodology used to investigate stress, coping styles and emotional control as a function of temperament among Type-A individuals. The description of methodology has been presented under five separate headings.

SAMPLE

The sample for the present study was drawn from the undergraduate students' population from various colleges of Bhiwani, Rohtak, Kurukshetra and Karnal district of Haryana State. Initially a total of 1841 students were taken as subjects for the study who were studying in B.A part I, II and III in Art, Science and Commerce faculties.

Since the subjects were required to be categorized into Type-A, Type-ABs and Type-Bs, first of all they were administered 21 items Type-A subscale of Jenkins Activity Survey. The subjects scoring above third quartile (Q_3 i.e., 252) were placed in Type-A group and those scoring below first quartile (Q_1 i.e., 170) in Type-B group. and also those who were between Q_1 and Q_3 were placed in Type-AB group. This criterion provided 281 individuals in each group. Others who did not respond were dropped from the final testing, thus the final sample came out to be of 843 individuals. The age of the subjects ranged between 17 to 22 years with a mean age of 18.39 years.

TEST MATERIALS USED

The following tests were used for the present study.

1. Stress Scale

Stress scale was drawn from Eight State Questionnaire designed by Cattell (1972), and adapted in India by Kapoor and Bhargava (1990), which measures eight important emotional states viz. anxiety, stress, depression, regression, fatigue, guilt, extraversion and arousal. Thus stress scale is one of the eight state scales of Eight State Questionnaire. This subscale comprising 12 items was used to assess the state of stress. According to Cattell, stress state means feeling a lot of pressure, unable to take time off and relax, constantly on the go, feeling hectic, experiencing great strain, unhappy with own performance, and experiencing lots of demands. The behavioral correlates of stress state in objective test domain are: "low motor and perceptual rigidity, better at memorizing meaningless material, high ratio of threatening objects seen in unstructured drawings".

The items of the scale can be answered using four alternate responses, thus preventing the subject to select a lazy middle category response. These alternate choices are very true, fairly true, fairly false and very false. The scale measures how subject feels now, at this moment. Form-B of the test was used which has test-retest reliability of 0.92 after a few hours interval. Validity of this state questionnaire is also substantial. The concept validity for Stress State (correlation of stress score with pure stress state factor) is 0.86.

2. Coping Style Questionnaire.

The coping style questionnaire – (CSQ) was initially developed by Roger in 1989, and was further revised by Roger et al. (1993) and adopted in India by Kaistha (2002). The CSQ is a 41-item questionnaire having four dimensions (factors): Rational coping, Detached coping, Emotional coping, and Avoidance coping. These four dimensions are grouped into maladaptive (Emotional and Avoidance coping) strategies and adaptive strategies (Rational and Detached). There are 9 items for rational coping, 9 items for detached coping, 10 items for avoidance coping and 13 items for emotional coping. Subject is to answer for each situation in either of the following ways: (a) always (b) often (c) seldom or (d) never. The four dimensions as measured by CSQ have operational meanings as given by Roger are:

a) Adaptive coping styles

i. Rational or Active coping means realistically accepting the stressful situation, without precluding the possibility of action. It is task oriented coping style with planning and rational thinking and represents adaptive coping style.

ii. Detached coping feeling of detachment does not involve denial or attempt to avoid stress (Roger, 1992). Subjects reported that the 'less involved' they felt with the event the more effectively they were able to cope. Detachment could be distinguished from task-oriented strategies but detachment is considered to be 'adaptive coping style'.

b) Maladaptive coping styles

i. Avoidance coping is considered as helplessness. It includes behavioural disengagement or giving up. It also includes denial. It is a negative kind of behaviour involving withdrawl and giving up.

ii. Emotional coping involves expressing feelings and seeking emotional support.

The test-retest reliability coefficients after an interval of 3 months, for combined sample were found to be substantial (Rational 0.80, Detached 0.79, Emotional 0.76 and Avoidance 0.70). The differences between separate retest correlations for male and female were negligible. The internal consistency coefficients as measured in terms of alpha coefficients were 0.85 for rational, 0.89 for detached, 0.73 for emotional and 0.69 for avoidance coping.

For concurrent validation of CSQ the scores were correlated with scores on Emotional Control Questionnaire-ECQ (Roger and Najarian, 1989). The tendency to ruminate on emotionally upsetting events (Rehearsal on ECQ) correlated significantly and positively with both of the maladaptive CSQ strategies (0.24 for avoidance coping and 0.51 for emotional coping), and significantly negatively correlated with both of the adaptive coping styles (-0.35 for rational coping and -0.48 for detached coping) (Briggs and Cheek, 1986).

3. Emotional control questionnaire.

Emotional Control Questionnaire (ECQ) was first constructed by Roger and Nesshoever in 1987 and finally validated by Roger and Najarian in 1989. They extracted four factors from the initial item pool. Earlier attempts to measure emotional response style were 'Picture Frustration study' developed by Rosenzweig, Fleming and Clarke (1947), but it has many problems regarding response classification and as usual with projective tests, its poor reliability and validity. The other measure used was 'Repression Sensitization (R-S) scale of Byrne (1961), which was derived from MMPI sub scales and is intended to provide an index of emotional expressiveness, but it is quite long and results are inconsistent. The scale has been adopted in India by Kaistha, Gupta and Darolia (2003) having very good psychometric properties.

Emotional control is defined as the tendency to inhibit the expression of emotional responses and the scale has been developed in context of research on role of personality/temperament as a moderator variable in the relationship between stress and illness. The four dimensions of emotional control questionnaire are based on factor analysis of initial item pool and all are internally consistent and stable over time. The four dimensions are: Rehearsal, Emotional inhibition, Aggression control and Benign control. Each factor has fourteen items, the full ECQ comprises of 56 items. Roger and Najarian's (1989) ECQ was used for the present study. The Kuder-Richardson reliabilities for the four factors assessed by the authors were found to be 0.86 for rehearsal, 0.77 for emotional inhibition, 0.79 for benign control and 0.81 for aggression control. The test-retest reliabilities for the four factors over a period of seven weeks interval were also substantial and satisfactory, 0.80 for rehearsal, 0.79 for emotional inhibition, 0.92 for benign control and 0.73 for aggression control.

For concurrent validation of ECQ the scores were correlated with scores on Eysenck's Personality Questionnaire-EPQ (Roger and Najarian, 1989). Rehearsal, correlated significantly with EPQ, N (0.57) and aggression control showed substantial negative correlation with neuroticism (-0.25). Extraversion was significantly and negatively correlated with emotional inhibition (-0.37), and correlation between extraversion and benign control was not significant, confirming that the scale is primarily a measure of impulsivity rather than sociability. Roger and Najarian (1989) described four scales as under:

a) Rehearsal measures the tendency to ruminate on emotionally upsetting events.

b) Emotional inhibition: measure the extent to which the expression of emotion is suppressed although the scale is independent of rehearsal, it has also shown some relationship to stress related physiological arousal.

c) Aggression control: reflects inhibition of hostility independently of the more general emotional restraints measured by emotional inhibition and the two scales are infact statistically unrelated.

d) Benign control: measures impulsiveness.

4. Formal Characteristics of Behavior – Temperament Inventory.

Guided by the postulates underlying the RTT and taking into account the state of affairs in diagnosing temperamental characteristics Strelau and Zawadzki (1993), developed the Formal Characteristics of Behavior Temperament Inventory, (FCB-TI) which fully corresponds with RTT especially, with the structure of temperament as proposed by the theory.   FCB – TI has a Yes/No answers format and is composed of six scales fully corresponding to the six temperamental traits postulated by the RTT:

a) Briskness: (BR) is tendency to react quickly to keep a high tempo of performing activities and to shift easily in response to changes in the surroundings from one behaviour to another.

b) Persistence: (PE) is tendency to continue and to repeat behaviour after cessation of stimuli (situation) evoking this behaviour.

c) Sensory sensitivity: (SS) is ability to react to sensory stimuli of low stimulative value.

d) Emotional Reactivity: (ER) is tendency to react intensively to emotion generating stimuli expressed in high emotional sensitivity and in low emotional endurance.

e) Endurance: (EN) is ability to react adequately in situations demanding long lasting or high stimulative activity and under intensive external stimulation.

f) Activity: (ACI) is tendency to undertake behaviour of high stimulative value or to supply by means of behaviour strong stimulation from the surroundings.

The temperament traits as measured by means of FCB-TI show satisfactory construct validity. The theoretically grounded location of RTT traits among other temperament constructs (PTS, EPQ-R, EASTS, DOTS-R, SSS-V) has been empirically verified. Correlations between Italian (DePascalis et al. 2000) and Polish version items range from .73 to .98, which are substantial and satisfactory. The original FCB-TI scale has an initial item pool of 381 items. It was initially adapted in Indian conditions by Rani and Darolia (2000). The Cronbach's coefficient alpha (reliability measure) for briskness (0.75), persistence (0.73), sensory sensitivity (0.76), emotional reactivity (0.78), endurance (0.74), and activity (0.61) are fairly satisfactory. The test has 112 items, divided into six domains on the basis of factor analysis conducted by the authors.

5. Jenkins Activity Survey.

Before selecting a scale for Type-A behavior pattern (TABP) scale, the investigator scanned fully the literature on Type-A behavior pattern and finally selected the widely used Jenkins Activity Survey (JAS). The Jenkins Activity Survey (Jenkins et al. 1979) is a four factor questionnaire which comprises Type-A behavior pattern (TABP) scale, the speed and impatience scale, the job involvement scale and the hard driving and competitive scale. For the selection of subjects on Type-A and Type-B behaviour pattern, the Type-A scale comprising 21 items was used for the present study. It is a paper pencil test with objective scoring. The 21 item TABP can be answered in a three or four category response (always, occasionally and never for three category response and extremely high, more, less, very few or definitely yes, probably yes, no and definitely no for four category response items). The TABP score is obtained by assessing weights associated with the marked option for each item in the scale. The single total score is obtained by summing up individual item scores.

Rosenman et al. (1975), referred to TABP as the hurry sickness and listed 13 characteristics that are most important trade marks for Type-A behaviour. Initially the structured interview (SI) was developed by Friedman and Rosenman (1974), which has 26 questions and measures TABP, but the major drawback was subjective nature of the technique, which demanded intensive training in scoring procedures. JAS is a self-reporting multiple-choice questionnaire. It is used in clinical settings and by researchers. It has been used by a number of investigators on Indian sample and proved a fair measure of TABP. The authors of JAS have reported very satisfactory reliability and validity estimates (Jenkins et al. 1979).

ADMINISTRATION OF TESTS

After identifying the three groups of individuals on the basis of scores on Jenkins activity survey i.e., Type-A, Type-AB and Type-Bs were administered four tests namely Formal Characteristics of Behavior Temperament Inventory (FCB-TI), Stress Questionnaire (SQ), Coping Style Questionnaire (CSQ) and Emotional Control Questionnaire (ECQ). The subjects were approached through heads of the institutions. The selected subjects were contacted in their respective classrooms in small groups ranging from 10 to 15 students, and their willingness to participate in the study was sought. Since most of the students were willing to participate in the testing only during their vacant periods, they were tested whenever they were ready to spare time for it. All the four tests were administered on 843 subjects (N = 281 for all three Type-A, AB and B groups) and their scores were processed for statistical analyses.

The testing was carried in a very congenial atmosphere. It was uniform all through out. Students were encouraged to respond in a realistic way without ruminating too much. The first, spontaneous response, they feel right, should be recorded on the questionnaire. A good rapport was established with the subjects in order to get real life setting results. They were told about the importance of the study and that the data collected will not be made public, rather confidentiality of their responses will be maintained. Subjects were informed that their position on different behavioral measures would be intimated to them if they so desire. Though there was no time limit, subjects were asked to complete the tests as early as possible. Subjects generally completed, SS in 10 to 15 minutes, CSQ in 30 to 35 minutes, and ECQ in 35 to 40 minutes. FCB-TI in 40 to 45 minutes. The instructions and administration procedures were same for all the subjects, and in accordance with that described by the test authors.

The sequence of presentation of the tests was stress scale, coping style questionnaire emotional control questionnaire and formal characteristics of behavior-temperament inventory. These tests were administered in different sessions keeping in view the time constraint.

Stress scale has twelve items with four response choices very true, true, false, and very false and out of these subjects are to select one choice, which she feels, represents her for most of the times,

Coping Style Questionnaire has 41 items with four alternate responses, always, often, seldom and never. Subject is supposed to select one out of these four responses, which she generally uses while reacting in different situations, which produce stress.

Emotional Control Questionnaire has 56 items with true/false pattern of response. Subject is to select either true or false presuming she is facing similar situation.

The FCB-TI is comprised of 112 items to be answered in Yes/No format, subjects were asked to cross inside the circle under heading Yes or No, keeping in mind, how they generally behave in different situations rather than how they should behave.

SCORING

For stress each item was scored 3, 2, 1 or 0. The high scoring direction was indicated by the letter a or d. If the letter was 'a' the 'a' response was scored 3 and the b response is scored 2 and the c response was scored 1. If the letter was a 'd' the d response was scored 3, the c response was scored 2, and the b response was scored 1. Thus scoring was in antagonistic manner.

Scoring for CSQ, detachment and emotional coping dimensions was done by assigning zero to always, 1 to often, 2 to some times and 3 to never. In just opposite manner scoring of rational and avoidance coping was done by assigning 3 to always, 2 to often, 1 to some times and 0 to never. The individual item scores for each domain were summed to obtain four different scores for four domains.

For Emotional Control Questionnaire scoring was done in form of one or zero. If the item was from true category and subject selected true choice, a score of one was given similarly, when the item was from the false category and the subject selected false choice, a score of one was given. But a score of zero was given to the subject when items was from true category and subject responded to it in a false manner or when the item was from the false category and subject selected a true response for it. Individual item scores were added dimension wise to obtain four scores for four domains i.e., rehearsal, benign control etc.

Scoring of FCB-T1 was done by using six scoring keys prepared for all the six dimensions of temperament also called formal characteristics of behavior i.e., briskness, perseverance, sensory sensitivity etc. In the case of FCB-T1 a score of '1'

was assigned to alpha responses and a score of '0' for other than alpha. Individual item scores were summed according to key to obtain six separate scores.